Published by Black Inc.
An imprint of Schwartz Publishing Pty Ltd
Level 5, 289 Flinders Lane
Melbourne Victoria 3000
Australia
61 3 9654 2000

Freeman, Meera, 1948- .
A season in Morocco.

Includes index.
ISBN 1 86395 363 9.

1. Cookery, Moroccan. 2. Morocco - Description and travel.
I. Payes, Sonia. II. Title.

641.5964

A Season in Morocco

A Culinary Journey

Meera Freeman

Photography by Meera Freeman and Sonia Payes

Table of Contents

Acknowledgements

I am grateful to all the people I have met during my travels in Morocco who have shared their knowledge, food and music with me.

Special thanks to Ahmed Nait and Fouad Belhaj of Travel Link, Marrakech for their unending generosity. To Seddik Aasim, my wonderful guide who knows everything and driver Khalid Benghozlane with whom I have covered thousands of kilometers and for whom nothing is too much trouble. Thanks too to Mohammed Azim and Mourad Chemsi who have also accompanied me on many an adventure.

To Abdel'adim Nejmeddine, my expert on street food and Moroccan music, and his family who have welcomed me into their homes and taught me quite a few culinary techniques.

Thanks go to the El Abbadi family whose riad La Maison Bleue is my home away from home in Fes – Abdeslam, Mehdi and Ghita, Kenza, Keltoum and Younes. Thank you all for your hospitality, pampering and exquisite food.

To the Alaoui Lamranis of La Maison Berbere in Rissani and Tinghir, heartfelt thanks for your hospitality, music and friendship, and for making buying carpets so painless.

I am grateful to all the hoteliers, restaurateurs and their staff who always make me and my groups so welcome and are always happy to cater to our every request.

In Australia, thanks to my family, friends and students for their love and support. Special thanks to Anna and Morry Schwartz, Caitlin and Luc Nation, Dorota Pytlewska and Driss Regague, official taster of my Moroccan dishes and definitely the greatest flatterer I know.

Thanks to Sophy Williams, Caitlin Yates and all the staff at Black Inc. for undertaking this project, to Allan Kleiman and David Lane for their design and production expertise and to Sonia Payes and Garry Smith for their photographs.

Mediterranean Sea

Tangiers
Ceuta (Sp.)
Asilah
Tetouan
Larache
Bou Ahmed
Al Hoceima
Melilla (Sp.)
El Amria
Beni Saf
Ksar el Kebir
Chaouen
Nador
Marsa Ben Mehidi
RIF MOUNTAINS
Midar
Ouezzane
Tlemcen
Souk-el-Arba El Gharb
Taounate
Aknoul
Oujda
Sebou
Sidi-Slimane
Taourirt
ALGERIA
Sebou
Kenitra
Sidi-Kacem
Volubilis
Taza
Guercif
El Aricha
Moulay Idriss
Fes
Âïn Benimathar
Meknes
Za
Abdelmoula
Khemisset
Sefrou
Charef
Rommani
Ifrane
ATLAS
Moulouya
Azrou
MOROCCO
Zerouilet
Borj de Trarite-Rhars-Allah
ZAËR ZAÏNE
Enjil
Outat Oulad al Haj
Matarka
Missour
Tendrara
Ghedir Draa El Rich
Kenifra
Oued Zem
MIDDLE
Anoual
Bouarfa
n Salah
Moulouya
Midelt
Talsinnt
Mengoub
Figuig
Beni Mellal
Amouguér
Âït Koujmane
Imilchil
Lahmar
Âït Mhammed
Er-Rachidia
Ksar-el-Azoudj
Tilmi
Boudenib
Guir
Todra Gorge
Goulmima
Béchar
ATLAS
Tinerhir
Touroug
Tinejdad
HAMADA
El Kelâa M'Gouna
Erfoud
Zousfana
O. Dades
Rissani
Merzouga
ALGERIA
Âït-Slilo
Abadia
DU
GUIR
Hamaguir
SAHARA
120 km / 75 miles

ix

List of Recipes All recipes serve 6 as part of a meal

Glossary

Argan (Argania Spinosa) – spiny-leafed tree native to southern Morocco that yields olive-like fruit from which oil is extracted.

Bastilla – famous Moroccan dish incorporating layers of pigeon, eggs and almonds in ouarqa pastry and sprinkled with superfine sugar and cinnamon.

Berber – a group of tribes living in North Africa and the Sahara.

Braewat – triangular pastries, savoury or sweet, covered in ouarqa pastry.

Chermoula – marinade made from pounded parsley and cilantro, garlic and paprika, lemon juice or vinegar. Used principally for marinating fish. Other ingredients can be added to make the chermoula more complex.

Couscous – pellets of grain made from durum wheat semolina and less often, barley or maize. The grain is steamed and eaten either in broth or dry. Of Berber origin, it is considered the national dish of Morocco.

Couscousier – two-tiered cooking vessel. The bottom part is used to cook broth whereas the top part is perforated. The couscous is cooked in the steam emanating from the bottom vessel.

Dirham – unit of currency in Morocco.

Djellabah – hooded overgarment worn by both men and women as street wear.

Foundouq – inn.

Ghassoul – pounded clay used primarily as a hair treatment.

Gnawa – musicians descended from black slaves transported in the late 17th and early 18th centuries from sub-Saharan Africa to serve as guards to the Sultans Moulay Ismail in Meknes and Moulay Abdallah in Essaouira. They venerated Bilal, the black Christian slave liberated by the Prophet Mohammed and who became the first muezzin – the one who calls the faithful to prayer. These musicians combine music and healing rituals, performing trance ceremonies that involve chanting and dancing, during which they invoke African Spirits and Muslim saints.

Hammam – Moorish bath house.

Kanoun – earthenware brazier which holds the coals over which the tajine cooks.

Kasbah – fortified dwelling.

Ksar – fortified village surrounded by walls and towers.

Maghreb – the land of the setting sun. The countries of North-West Africa including Morocco, Algeria Tunisia and Libya.

Medina – traditional Arab walled city.

Mellah – Jewish quarter within an Arab medina.

Ouarqa – pastry made by dabbing a piece of dough onto a hot surface to form a paper-thin layer. Used in bastilla, braewat and other filled pastries.

Oud – string instrument similar to a mandolin, traditionally used in playing Andalusian music.

Oued – river.

Ras el Hanout – literally 'top of the shop' – a mixture of spices sometimes containing more than forty ingredients.

Riad – walled garden – now common term for a private house/hotel built around an internal garden.

Smen – salted and aged butter, sometimes flavored with herbs.

Souq – market.

Tadelakt – a waterproof render made from Marrakech limestone, often tinted with natural pigments and used in various applications, especially on the walls of traditional Moorish baths.

Tajine – earthenware cooking vessel with a tapered lid. Also the name given to dishes cooked in this vessel.

Zelij – intricate geometric mosaic made from pieces of tile and widely used on walls, floors and table tops, particularly in Fes.

The Moroccan Kitchen

Utensils

Berad – Moroccan teapot made from metal.

Couscousier – two-tiered metal pot, used for steaming couscous.

Gsaa – wooden or earthenware vessel used for making dough or preparing couscous.

Mehraz – mortar and pestle, usually made from brass, used for pounding spices and almonds for pastries.

Tajine – earthenware vessel with conical lid in which Moroccan stews are cooked.

Tobsil dyal ouarqa – a copper vessel used upside down over a heat source and on which dough is tapped to form the thin sheets of pastry.

Herbs and Spices most commonly used in Moroccan cooking

Spices

Cumin	cuminum cyminum	kamoun
Cinnamon	cinnamomum zeylanicum	dar el cini
Cassia	cinnamomum cassia	qarfa
Ginger	zingiber officinale	skinjbir
Sweet paprika	bell pepper annuum	flefla hilwa
Hot paprika	bell pepper minimum	flefla harra
Hot chillies	bell pepper sp.	flefla soudaniya
Black pepper	piper nigrum	l'bzar
Saffron	crocus sativus	za'afran
Anise	pimpinella anisum	nafaa (mainly in pastries)
Sesame seeds	sesamum indicum	jenjelan

Ras el Hanout or **'top of the shop'** is a blend of exotic spices which can contain anything from ten to fifty spices. It generally includes ginger, turmeric, cardamom, long pepper, cubebe pepper, cassia bark, nutmeg, mace, ash berries, allspice and grains of paradise.

Aromatic Herbs for cooking

Onion	allium cepa	bsla
Garlic	allium sativum	touma
Cilantro	coriandrum sativum	kousbour
Parsley	carum petroselinum	madnouss

Herbs for infusion as tea

Mint	mentha viridis	na'ana
Lemon Verbena	lippia citriodora	louisa
Pennyroyal	mentha pulegium	fliou
Marjoram	origanum marjorana	merddedouch
Rose Geranium	pelargonium roseum	laatrache
Sage	salvia officinalis	salmiya
Wormwood	artemisia absinthium	chiba

Distilled flower waters

Orange blossom water distilled from Seville orange blossoms	zhar
Rosewater distilled from damask roses	ma ouard

Olives, preserved lemons and sauces in a market stall

The Basics

Fresh Tomato Sauce

4 fresh ripe tomatoes, blanched and seeded

salt

1 tsp freshly squeezed lemon juice

1 tsp finely chopped parsley

Push the tomatoes through a sieve to obtain a dense puree. Add the salt, lemon juice and parsley and stir to combine. Serve with grilled meats.

Smen

Salted or herbed, aged butter used in tajines, pancakes and to give couscous a unique flavor.

It is difficult to replicate the flavour if making smen with pasteurized butter. Commercial ghee can be used to achieve a similar taste.

Harissa Sauce

10 dried red chillies, seeded, sliced and soaked

4 large cloves garlic

$\frac{1}{2}$ tsp salt

$\frac{1}{2}$ tsp cumin

In a mortar grind the garlic, salt and cumin to a fine paste.

Drain the chillies and chop them as finely as possible with a heavy knife.

Transfer to the mortar and pound until a fine red paste is achieved.

Dilute with hot water or stock and serve as a condiment for couscous.

or

Mix with extra virgin olive oil and serve as a dip for bread.

COUSCOUS

1 lb medium couscous grains

1 tsp salt

1 tbsp olive oil or butter

Pour the couscous grains into a fine strainer and rinse them under running water, allowing all the excess water to drain off.

Spread the moistened grains out onto a flat tray and sprinkle with the salt. Leave to swell for about 5 minutes.

Roll the couscous between the palms of your hands to break up the mass that will have formed and separate and aerate the grains. Transfer the worked couscous to a steamer and steam over boiling water for 20 minutes.

Remove from the steamer and return to the tray. Break up any lumps that may have formed with a fork. Sprinkle with a $\frac{1}{2}$ cup cold water.

When cool enough to handle, roll again between the palms of your hands to ensure that the grains are well separated and return to the steamer for a further 15 minutes.

Repeat this process, adding the olive oil or butter to the grains before steaming for a final 15 minutes.

PRESERVED LEMONS

1 dozen untreated freshly picked lemons

coarse sea salt

juice of 4 lemons

Wash the lemons and leave them to soak in cold water for 3 days, changing the water every day. At the end of this time, dry the lemons and cut them in quarters, leaving them attached at one end.

Pour a thin layer of salt into the bottom of a sterilized jar. Sprinkle more salt into the flesh of the lemons and press the quarters together to reform the whole fruit. Put them into the jar, sprinkling with more sea salt and pressing them down into the jar.

When all the lemons have been salted and put in the jar, place a weight on top of them and fill the jar to the brim with lemon juice.

Seal and leave in a cool, dark place for a month before using. If the level of liquid should decrease, top up with boiled water and re-seal.

OUARQA

Ouarqa is the name given to circular, paper-thin sheets of pastry obtained by repeatedly tapping a ball of dough onto the surface of a hot pan. They are used for making both sweet and savory parcels, which are then fried, and the famous bastilla – the masterpiece of Moroccan cuisine.

Making ouarqa requires a good deal of experience even though the dough itself is simple to prepare.

Both Robert Carrier and Kitty Morse (see Recommended Reading, Page 206) give simplified methods where a liquid batter is prepared and painted onto the hot surface instead of using the dabbing method that requires years of practice to perfect. Quite satisfactory results can be obtained by substituting commercially available Greek filo pastry leaves in recipes specifying ouarqa.

8 oz plain flour

8 oz fine semolina

large pinch of salt

water

Sift both types of flour together with the salt. Add enough water to obtain a firm dough and knead until it is supple and elastic. Add more water, a little at a time and continue to knead until a soft, almost liquid dough is obtained.

To verify the correct consistency, try taking a little of the dough, letting it drop and catching it as it falls. It should spring up like the movement of a yoyo.

Knead it for a few more minutes, lifting the dough and dropping it back onto the work surface several times.

Put the finished dough into a bowl and just cover it with water. Leave it to rest for an hour or so before using.

Place the tobsil dyal ouarqa upside down over a pot of boiling water or over a medium gas flame making sure that the heat is evenly distributed. Lightly oil the pan.

Wet your fingers and take a little of the dough, dabbing it lightly all over the surface of the pan, letting it drop and pulling it up with a yoyo-like motion, until a fine layer is formed. Peel it off the pan and place on a cloth, shiny side up. Make more sheets of ouarqa in the same manner until all the dough is used up, piling them on top of each other and covering with another cloth as soon as they are ready.

Forecourt, Hassan II mosque

1

Casablanca

La Fibule Restaurant

Douira Restaurant

Above Left *Grid for displaying electoral candidates on public building*
Above Centre *Unloading bread*
Above Right *Roses, Royal Mansour*
Below *Foyer Royal Mansour Hotel*

2

Our aircraft touched down at Casablanca airport on time after our thirty-hour journey from Melbourne. It was astonishing to think that we had just crossed the entire African continent from east to west. Although tired, we were excited and full of anticipation as we were met by our guide and driver who would take care of us over the following two weeks.

It was mid-afternoon by the time we arrived at the luxurious Royal Mansour hotel. After a quick shower, we assembled in the courtyard for a glass of fragrant mint tea before setting out for a walk in the walled city just across the road. I couldn't resist buying a few loaves of warm wholemeal bread from a vendor just inside the gate – our first taste of Morocco. We walked for an hour or so through the streets of the medina watching the children playing in the narrow streets and admiring the architecture. We continued outside the city walls and strolled down to the port enjoying the breeze coming in from the sea and arrived back at the hotel with an hour or so to spare before dinner.

Khalid, our driver, collected us at dusk and headed for the Corniche – Casablanca's famous coastal esplanade – passing the spectacular Hassan II mosque whose lofty silhouette we could just make out through the evening mist. We drove the whole length of the Corniche, in turn admiring the coastline and groaning with dismay at the all too familiar neon signs that marred this beautiful scenic route, before alighting for a preprandial stroll.

Our first gastronomic experience was to take place at La Fibule restaurant on the sea at Ain Diab, close to the old lighthouse.

The restaurant was decorated in traditional Moroccan style with lime-washed walls, carved plaster friezes and elaborate woodwork. Aziz, the Maitre d'hotel, welcomed us and seated us at a round table where wrinkled black olives and green spiced olives had been set out alongside a bowl of Aziz's own special hot sauce made from fresh hot peppers, vinegar and olive oil. These offerings, with Moroccan bread, prepared our tastebuds for what was to follow.

First came a seafood bastilla – a modern variation on the classic pigeon and egg extravaganza. This one consisted of thin leaves of ouarqa pastry filled with a combination of Chinese jelly noodles, mushrooms, seafood, herbs and spices, and fried to crispy succulence. Everyone declared it to be the best thing they had ever eaten in their lives – a phrase I was to hear over and over again.

Next a great tajine of veal shanks garnished with hard-boiled eggs and almonds was served. This festive dish, known as tfaya, is generally made for weddings and other celebrations. Our token vegetarian was offered couscous with seven vegetables accompanied by a bowl of sweet onion jam with golden raisins. She (and the others) found it so delicious that they were soon begging for another serving.

Above Left *Tomb of holy woman, Lalla Taja*
Above Centre *Fresh bread*
Above Right *Water vendor's hat*

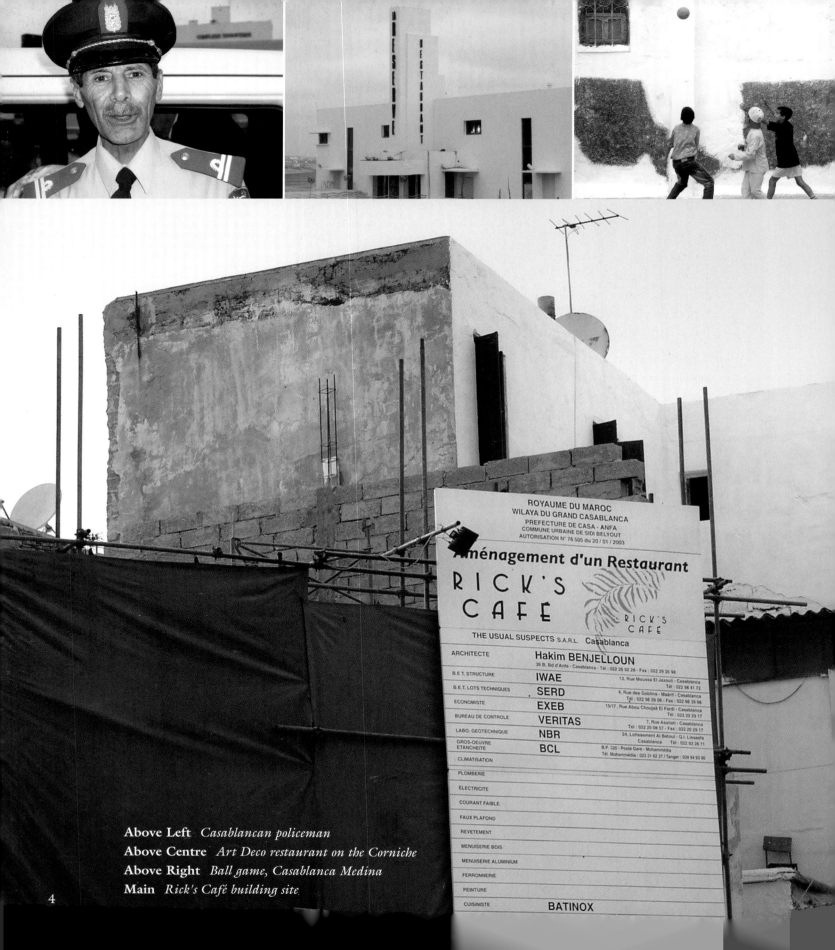

Above Left *Casablancan policeman*
Above Centre *Art Deco restaurant on the Corniche*
Above Right *Ball game, Casablanca Medina*
Main *Rick's Café building site*

4

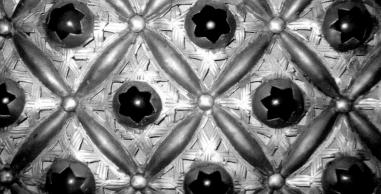

We ate surrounded by the strains of haunting songs of Andalusia and soulful Jewish melodies from the 14th century performed by a handsome musician dressed in an exquisite cream caftan, his fine features appearing as though carved from ebony.

Thin slices of apple and the last plums of the season were served in rosewater syrup and the meal ended with a pot of mint tea and a plate of some of the most delicious pastries I have ever tasted. Surely they must have been the work of an experienced cook who had perfected her technique over an entire lifetime. I asked to meet the genie who had produced these works of art. To my amazement, a very young girl called Mina emerged from the kitchens to receive our compliments.

It was still quite early but we were tired from our flight and drowsy from the wonderful meal. Khalid was waiting to drive us back to the hotel for a good night's sleep with dreams perfumed with the scent of spices and rosewater.

AZIZ'S HARISSA

20 large fresh red chillies, seeded

$\frac{1}{2}$ tsp salt

juice of one lemon

2 tbsp vinegar

3 tbsp olive oil

Blend the chillies, salt and lemon juice together in a blender to obtain a thick paste.

Beat in the vinegar and olive oil making quite a liquid mixture. Taste for salt and adjust the seasoning if necessary. This hot sauce can be kept in a jar in the refrigerator and used as a condiment, to spice olives or as an ingredient in salads and other dishes.

Above Left *Oud player, La Fibule*
Above Centre *Detail, La Fibule*
Above Right *Pouring tea, La Fibule*

Seafood Bastilla

1 x 3 oz packet Chinese cellophane noodles

2 tbsp dried Chinese black fungus, reconstituted in water

2 tbsp vegetable oil

3 cloves garlic, finely chopped

4 oz small firm champignon mushrooms, sliced

1 medium squid, cleaned and cut into small squares

8 oz fresh shrimp, each cut into 3 pieces

8 oz white fish fillet, cut into small pieces

1 tsp salt

1 tsp ground ginger

large pinch saffron

large pinch freshly ground black pepper

juice of $\frac{1}{2}$ lemon

$\frac{1}{4}$ cup chopped cilantro leaves

$\frac{1}{4}$ cup chopped flat leaf parsley

10 sheets ouarqa pastry or $\frac{1}{2}$ packet filo pastry

1 egg yolk

Soak the cellophane noodles in hot (not boiling water) for 10 minutes until they have softened.

Drain and cut into short lengths. Drain the black fungus and chop it into small pieces.

In a large frying pan, heat the oil with the garlic and as soon as the garlic begins to soften, add the champignons and sauté until they render their juices and begin to brown. Add the fish fillet, the squid and the shrimp and sauté until just cooked through. Off the heat, add the noodles, black fungus, the salt, spices, lemon juice, cilantro and parsley and stir well to combine. Transfer the mixture to a colander and allow it to drain and cool.

Brush a round tray with a little vegetable oil and spread out 4 sheets of pastry, allowing them to overlap and hang over the edge of the tray. Place another sheet on top. (If using filo pastry, lightly brush each sheet with oil as you go.) Pile the seafood mixture into the centre of the prepared pastry sheets and cover them with the remaining pastry sheets, tucking the edges under to form a round pie shape.

Brush the top of the pie with the beaten egg yolk and bake in a 350°F Gas Mark 4 oven until golden brown.

Alternatively, omit the egg yolk glaze and fry the pie gently in a heavy frying pan until golden brown. Turn and fry the other side.

Turn out and serve hot.

Tajine of Veal Tfaya

2 large onions

3 lb veal shanks, cut across into 3 pieces each

1 tbsp butter

2 tbsp vegetable oil

1 bunch fresh cilantro, chopped

1 tsp salt

1 tsp freshly ground black pepper

1 tsp ground ginger

1 large pinch saffron

1 piece cassia bark

1 cup water

8 oz blanched almonds, fried in oil or
toasted in the oven until golden

6 hard boiled eggs

Peel the onions and chop them finely. Put them in an earthenware casserole together with the veal shanks, butter, oil, coriander, salt and spices. Add the water, cover and bring to the boil.

Lower the heat and simmer for 1–1½ hours until the meat is tender. Uncover and cook until the sauce is thick and reduced.

Serve garnished with the almonds and the eggs, cut in half.

10

Gazelles' Horns

Dough

8 oz all purpose flour

$\frac{1}{2}$ oz softened butter

2 tbsp orange blossom water

1 egg yolk

Filling

8 oz ground almonds

$5\frac{1}{2}$ oz superfine sugar

2 drops almond essence

4 tbsp orange blossom water

Work the butter into the flour with your fingers or place the flour and butter in a food processor and pulse until the mixture resembles coarse breadcrumbs.

Add the orange blossom water and egg yolk and work or pulse until the dough comes together into a ball. Knead briefly and cover with an upturned bowl to rest while preparing the filling.

Put the ground almonds into a bowl. Sift the superfine sugar over them, add the almond essence and stir to mix well. Add the orange blossom water and mix with your hands, kneading until the mixture comes together and a smooth, dense paste is obtained. Pinch off walnut-sized pieces of paste. Roll them into lengths of about $2\frac{1}{2}$ inches, tapering towards each end.

Divide the dough into 4 pieces and working with the first piece, roll the dough into a paper thin sheet 4 in by 20 in. This can be most easily done using a pasta machine.

Place the lengths of filling in a row on the bottom third of the dough strip leaving some space between them. Stretch the dough back over the filling and cut between the lengths of filling.

Take each pastry and seal the edges together, either crimping with the tines of a fork or pressing down with your fingers. Bend each pastry into a crescent shape and pinch the pastry up to form a ridge on the top, thus expelling most of the air inside. Prick each crescent in several places with a pin or cake tester and make sure that the edges are well sealed so that they do not split during baking and let the filling ooze out. Bake in a moderate oven (350°F Gas Mark 4) for 20 minutes or until pale gold. Cool and store in an airtight box.

Fekkas

1 sachet ($\frac{1}{4}$ oz) active dry yeast

$\frac{1}{2}$ tsp sugar

13 oz all purpose flour

1 tsp salt

4 oz superfine sugar

$\frac{1}{2}$ oz melted butter

1 tsp mastic pounded with 1 tsp white sugar

pinch salt

3 tbsp orange blossom water

2 tbsp warm water

1 tbsp anise seeds

2 tbsp toasted sesame seeds

Dissolve the yeast and the sugar in 4 tbsp warm water and set aside for 5 minutes until it bubbles.

Make a soft dough with half the quantity of flour, all the salt and the yeast mixture, adding a little more water until the desired consistency is achieved.

Turn the dough out onto a floured surface and knead for about 10 minutes until smooth and elastic.

Form it into a ball, place in a floured bowl, cover with a cloth and set aside to rise for 1–2 hours or until doubled in size.

Add the remaining flour and the rest of the ingredients and knead for a further 10–15 minutes until the dough is smooth and elastic. Divide the dough into 5 portions. On a floured surface, roll each portion into a long roll about half an inch in diameter. Place on a tray lined with baking paper leaving room between the rolls to allow for spreading and rising. Cover with a cloth and set aside to rise for a further 1–2 hours.

Preheat the oven to 320°F.

Prick the rolls with the tines of a fork at regular intervals and place in the oven. Bake for approx. 10 minutes until the rolls are partially cooked. Do not allow them to brown.

Transfer from the oven to a rack to cool. When completely cold, cover with a cloth and set aside till the next day.

The following day, cut the rolls with a bread knife into diagonal slices about a third of an inch thick.

Place the slices in one layer on a baking tray and dry them out in a 300°F Gas Mark 2 oven until they become crisp and golden brown. Once cool, they will keep for quite a long time in an airtight container.

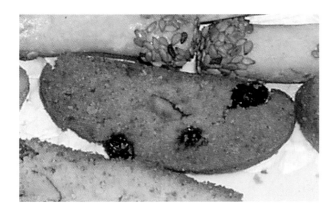

Above Left *Yoghurt with fresh fruit*
Above Centre *Breakfast breads*
Above Right *Zahira cooking msammen*
Below *French pastries*

14

The next morning I rose early and went down to the hotel courtyard for a glass of juice, freshly squeezed from Morocco's famous oranges. Soon the rest of our party straggled in and proceeded to fill their plates from the buffet table laden with Moroccan and Western dishes. Moroccan doughnuts and breakfast breads as well as a selection of French pastries were piled into baskets. At the far end of the courtyard, an attractive plump woman named Zahira prepared flaky flatbread called msammen and crumpet-like pancakes called beghrir which she cooked in skillets and drenched in butter for the hungry guests. On one of the tables, there were ceramic bowls of varietal honeys scented with field flowers, orange blossoms or eucalyptus to drizzle over the warm breakfast breads.

We would have needed to stay at the hotel for a whole week to take advantage of the variety of delicacies on offer. French coffee, espresso or mint tea were on offer and we all overindulged before disappearing into our rooms to get ready for the morning's outing.

Our tour started with a visit to the Hassan II mosque overlooking the sea and whose outline we had just been able to make out through the haze the previous evening.

Opened in 1993 to celebrate the King's sixtieth birthday, it is one of the very few mosques in Morocco where entry is permitted to non-Muslims. In size, it is second only to the great mosque in Mecca with room for 25,000 faithful in its immense prayer hall. Its 650 foot high minaret projects laser beams twenty miles in the direction of Mecca. There is a virtual forest of ornate marble ablution fonts downstairs for ritual washing before prayer and every detail is perfect. Although the mosque was designed by a French architect, Michel Pinseau, the complete panoply of Morocco's arts and crafts is represented here and everything, bar a little Carrrara marble and the Italian chandeliers, has made use of the country's own resources. Carved plaster, tadelakt stucco, zelij tilework, painted and carved cedar as well as marble and other stone from various parts of Morocco have been lovingly worked and applied by some 35,000 craftsmen.

The adjoining public baths and pools have not as yet been put to use, purportedly because of the enormous cost involved in firing up the furnaces and maintaining the services. The mosque with its outbuildings is one of the absolute must-sees of the city as much for its scale as the lavishness of its appointments and one can only marvel at its breathtaking splendor.

Our morning was filled with more wonderful sights as we set off for a drive through the prestigious suburb of Anfar, set in the highest part of Casablanca. White houses were hidden behind high walls dripping with multicolored bougainvillea, uniformed watchmen keeping guard outside.

We drove back to town admiring the Art Deco architecture and stopping at the Notre Dame de Lourdes cathedral, built by the French, with its grotto and stunning wall of stained glass by the artist Gabriel Loire of Chartres.

Above Left   *Orange juice*
Above Centre   *Oranges*
Above Right   *Zelij detail, Hassan II mosque*

16

We made our way to the Quartier des Habous, the modern medina built by the French. This is the site of the Royal Palace and government buildings as well as the French Consulate with its bronze statue of General Lyautey, the first French Governor of Morocco who was responsible for the wide boulevards and modern architecture in the kingdom's principal towns.

Our tour ended at the European food markets, another legacy of the colonial era, where we were surprised to see such a wide range of French goods. There were herbs such as tarragon, rosemary and chervil which are not normally used in the indigenous cuisine, as well as a French 'boucherie chevaline', horse butchery which had everyone screwing up their faces and tut-tutting.

Our tour of the market terminated in the fish section. We stopped at a stall where oysters from Oualidia that had been packed and shipped that morning were displayed on a bed of fennel leaves and pale pink rose petals.

The stall holder shucked them and squeezed drops of lemon juice onto them before handing them to us for on the spot consumption. They were so fresh and delicious that we must have eaten two or three dozen.

Seddik, our guide, and I bought a sea bass for each of us and a kilo of tiny shrimp from a stall recommended by the oyster lady. We delivered them to a café in the courtyard adjoining the market where they would be cooked and we then set off in search of olives and some fruit for our dessert.

On our return, a table had been set and the olives we had bought soon arrived together with fresh tomato and spicy harissa sauces and baskets of warm French and Moroccan breads. We were each served a salad of tomatoes, cucumber, red onion and baby lettuces, simply dressed with olive oil and lemon. This reminded us how real tomatoes should taste! The salad was followed by our fish – cleaned, scored, dipped in flour and quickly fried – and a pile of the pink boiled shrimp garnished with chopped parsley and lemon wedges. The waiter brought us a small dish of damp, grey sea salt that looked as though it had just been gathered from a local beach – the perfect accompaniment to the fish. We finished our lunch with the fruit and mandatory pot of mint tea and walked back to the hotel for an afternoon nap.

In the evening, we met for dinner at the Douira, the Royal Mansour's Moroccan restaurant, beautifully fitted out in traditional style with decorative plaster ceilings painted in pastel colors and walls clad in blue, green and white zelij mosaics. The room was divided into private seating areas by carved cedar screens, its walls lined with plush divans piled with soft cushions. Round tables were placed in front of the divans and dressed with golden beige cloths, completely covered in red cross-stitch motifs. Matching table napkins were weighted in one corner to stop them from falling off one's lap.

Opposite Page *Interior, Hassan II mosque*

Above Left *Detail, Hassan II mosque*
Above Centre *Court, Hassan II mosque*
Above Right *Ablution fonts*

The room was softly lit by beaten brass lanterns and occasional lamps with silk shades.

At the entrance, the Maitre d' poured orange blossom-scented water from a silver ewer over each guest's hands into a silver bowl. Fresh towels were provided and we were led to our table. As we pondered the menu, small bowls of spiced green olives and marinated sardines were offered to whet our appetites.

The meal began with two kinds of braewat pastries filled with meat or sardines and a selection of Moroccan salads – tomato and cucumber, carrot, beetroot, eggplant, green pepper, and cauliflower – served with round loaves of Moroccan bread. A bastilla followed, stuffed with large pieces of fish and seafood. It contained spinach as well as the jelly noodles we had encountered the night before. The filling was quite delicious and the pastry very good, although the gossamer ouarqa made by Mina at La Fibule was a hard act to follow.

Two tajines were served after the bastilla, one of marinated monkfish with green olives, red peppers and preserved lemon and the other of country chicken with onions, preserved lemons and violet-colored olives.

The fish tajine could only be described as orgasmic, the magical combination of the parsley and coriander melding with the saffron, paprika and cumin to create a kaleidoscope of flavors in every mouthful.

We selected our first bottle of Moroccan wine, a Medaillon Cabernet Sauvignon 2000 from the Meknes region, which was soft and mellow and did not overwhelm the delicate seasoning of the dishes.

As we ate and drank, imbibing the exotic atmosphere of the room, we were serenaded by a very fine musician playing the oud and a beautiful young woman dressed in a black caftan who sang in Arabic.

The party of Egyptian ladies at the next table was most appreciative and joined in the singing.

The evening was drawing to a close and we were feeling replete and drowsy by the time dessert was served. This consisted of a plate of sliced oranges sprinkled with sugar and cinnamon and crowned with a scoop of orange sorbet alongside a mound of seff'a – fine couscous – steamed with butter, perfumed with sugar and cinnamon and encircled by golden fried almonds. A jug of frothed milk infused with cinnamon was offered to moisten the couscous.

After dessert, the waiter sprinkled orange blossom water on our hands from a special silver dispenser.

Mint tea, this time perfumed with a few drops of orange blossom water to help us sleep, was served with three irresistible kinds of pastries – gazelles' horns, ghriba and almond and sesame fingers. We virtually rolled out of the restaurant. It was a blessing that our rooms were not far away.

Above Left *Oyster vendor*
Above Centre *Shucking oysters*
Above Right *Fried fish*

Opposite Page *Alfresco lunch, Casablanca market*

19

SPICED CARROT PUREE

1 lb young carrots

2 cloves garlic, finely chopped

1 pint water

1 tbsp olive oil

1 tbsp lemon juice

$\frac{1}{2}$ tsp sweet paprika

$\frac{1}{2}$ tsp powdered cumin

salt

freshly ground black pepper

2 tbsp chopped flat leaf parsley

Peel the carrots and cut into pieces.

Bring the water to the boil and simmer the carrots together with the garlic for 10–15 minutes, or until tender. Drain the carrots and garlic.

Heat the oil in a frying pan and add the carrots and garlic mashing them to a coarse puree. Stir in the lemon juice, paprika and cumin. Add salt and pepper to taste. Remove from heat and allow to cool to room temperature. Garnish with the parsley.

Salad of Cooked Beetroot

2 lb beetroot

salt to taste

1 tsp sugar

1 tsp powdered cumin

1 tsp orange blossom water

juice of $\frac{1}{2}$ lemon

olive oil

Bake the beetroot in a moderate oven until they are tender. (This method of cooking will prevent them from losing their color).

When cooked, remove from oven and allow to cool a little before peeling.

Cut the peeled beetroot into cubes and season with salt, sugar and cumin.

Stir in the orange blossom water and lemon juice and just enough olive oil to coat the beetroot. Serve at room temperature.

CHICKEN WITH LEMON AND OLIVES

8 chicken thighs, with bone

2 chicken livers

1 tsp salt

2 cloves garlic, sliced

1 tsp ground ginger

1 tsp sweet paprika

large pinch cumin

large pinch freshly ground black pepper

3 tbsp olive oil

1 onion, grated and squeezed dry

large pinch powdered saffron

handful chopped cilantro and parsley

1 cup brown or violet olives

2 preserved lemons

juice of 1 fresh lemon

In a bowl, combine the salt, garlic, ginger, paprika, cumin, pepper and oil and marinate the chicken pieces and livers in this mixture for an hour or so.

Place the chicken with its marinade in a casserole together with half the grated onion, the saffron, chopped herbs and $\frac{1}{2}$ cup water. Bring to the boil and simmer for about 30 minutes turning the chicken from time to time.

In the meantime, pit the olives. If they are bitter, boil them in water for 2 minutes and drain.

After the 30 minutes, remove the livers from the casserole and mash them to a fine pulp. Return to the casserole with the rest of the grated onion and cook for another 20 minutes, adding more water if necessary.

Rinse the preserved lemons and discard the pulp, cutting the peel into thin strips.

Add the olives and lemons to the casserole and cook for another 5 minutes or so. Remove the chicken, lemons and olives to a serving dish and reduce the sauce over a high flame adding the fresh lemon juice and salt to taste.

Pour over the chicken and serve hot.

Tajine of Fish M'Chermel

2 lb thick fish fillets (trevally or blue eye)

2 tomatoes, peeled, seeded and chopped

1 red bell pepper, grilled, peeled and seeded

3 tbsp parsley, finely chopped

peel of 1 preserved lemon, cut into strips

$\frac{1}{4}$ cup cracked green olives

Chermoula

$\frac{1}{2}$ cup cilantro leaves

$\frac{1}{2}$ cup parsley leaves

1 tsp powdered cumin

1 tsp salt

3 tbsp lemon juice

harissa to taste (optional)

To make the chermoula, pound the garlic in a mortar with the herbs, salt and spices. Stir in the lemon juice and the optional harissa.

Marinate the fish in half of the chermoula for at least 2 hours.

Pit the olives and set aside.

Cut the bell pepper into 6 to 8 pieces.

Place the fish with its marinade into a clean pan with the remaining chermoula, the tomatoes and the pepper pieces.

Cook covered for about 5 minutes or until the fish is almost cooked through. Stir in the preserved lemon peel and olives and cook for a further 5 minutes.

Serve hot or cold.

Seff'a

1 lb fine couscous

water

2 large pinches salt

$3\frac{1}{2}$ oz butter

1 cup golden raisins

1 cup blanched almonds

1 cup superfine sugar

1 tbsp ground cinnamon

1 cup milk

1 cinnamon stick

Pour the couscous grains into a fine strainer and rinse them under running water, allowing all the excess water to drain off.

Spread the moistened grains out onto a flat tray and sprinkle with the salt. Leave to swell for about 5 minutes.

Roll the couscous between the palms of your hands to break up the mass that will have formed and to separate and aerate the grains. Transfer the worked couscous to a steamer and steam over boiling water for 20 minutes.

Turn the couscous out onto the tray and add $\frac{1}{3}$ of the butter, sprinkling with about $\frac{1}{4}$ cup more water.

Loosen the grains with a fork and separate the couscous grains with your hands as soon as they are cool enough to handle.

Steam for a further 15 minutes.

Turn out the couscous again and add an extra $\frac{1}{3}$ of the butter and another $\frac{1}{4}$ cup water. Steam for another 10 minutes.

While the couscous is steaming, fry the blanched almonds in extra butter or toast in the oven and chop coarsely.

Turn out the couscous and toss with the remaining butter. Sprinkle with $\frac{1}{2}$ cup of the sugar, stirring to combine.

Heat the milk with the cinnamon stick and keep warm, leaving to infuse for 10 minutes.

Steam the golden raisins for 5 minutes and stir through the couscous.

Pile the couscous in a pyramid onto a serving dish. Cover with a cap of superfine sugar and decorate with stripes of cinnamon. Distribute the almonds around the circumference.

Serve with a jug of the warm cinnamon-flavoured milk for each guest to moisten his or her serving of couscous as desired.

ORANGES WITH CINNAMON

6 oranges

1 tbsp superfine sugar

1 tsp ground cinnamon

Peel and slice the oranges and arrange them in one layer on a flat plate.

Sprinkle with the sugar and cinnamon and serve.

ALMOND AND SESAME FINGERS

1 lb almond meal

½ lb superfine sugar

1 tbsp orange blossom water

1 tbsp melted butter

4 oz toasted sesame seeds

Mix the almond meal and the sugar together and, adding the orange blossom water and the melted butter, knead it into a firm paste.

Break off walnut-sized pieces and roll them into finger shapes.

Roll them in the sesame seeds, pressing down to make sure that the fingers are completely covered in seeds. Place carefully on a baking sheet covered in baking paper and bake for 15 minutes at 350°F Gas Mark 4. Remove from the oven, allow to cool and store in an airtight box.

GHRIBA

8 oz all purpose flour

4 oz fine semolina

4 oz superfine sugar

1 oz softened butter

Sift the flour, semolina and superfine sugar together in a food processor. Add the butter and process until the mixture comes together and forms a ball.

Pinch off walnut-sized pieces and roll them into balls.

Flatten slightly and place on a paper-lined baking sheet.

Bake at 350°F Gas Mark 4 for 10–15 minutes or until pale gold.

Allow to cool before storing in an airtight tin.

Royal guards, Rabat

2

Rabat

FRIED MARINATED FISH

COUSCOUS WITH FISH IN
SAFFRON

Above Left   *School excursion to Royal Mausoleum*
Above Centre   *Hassan tower*
Above Right   *Reconstructed pillars*
Below   *Guard, Royal Mausoleum*

Rabat is situated on the North Atlantic coast and sits on the southern bank of the Bou Regreg river opposite its sister city Sale. It was built on the ruins of the Roman town of Sala Colonia and, for about 300 years, was home to the notorious Sale pirates who plundered European trading vessels until the early 19th century.

The French protectorate made Rabat its administrative capital in 1912 and built a new town with wide boulevards and green parks adjacent to the medina that the Almohad sultan, Yakoub ben Mansour had founded in the 12th century.

Our first stop was a visit to the ruins of the Hassan Tower, the incomplete minaret of ben Mansour's project to build the largest mosque in all of Islam. He died four years after embarking on the works and so the mosque was never completed. An earthquake in 1755 leveled most of the existing construction but the tower still stands, dominating the river. Many of the fallen columns have recently been re-erected on the imposing site.

We continued to the adjacent mausoleum of Mohammed V that was built in the 1960s and houses the remains of two recent rulers of the Alaouite dynasty, Mohammed V and his son Hassan II as well as other members of the royal family. Several hundred Moroccan artisans were employed to decorate the mausoleum and the zelij work is some of the most intricate and beautiful I have seen. Royal guards, splendid in their white summer uniforms, stood guard at the entrance to the crypt whilst others on horseback formed a sentry at the gates to the complex. A group of children on a school excursion, assembled outside with their teacher after paying their respects at the royal tombs.

Our next stop was the Kasbah des Oudaias, a quarter in the highest part of the walled city overlooking the estuary and the Atlantic ocean. We entered the kasbah through a magnificent Almohad gate and, as we wandered through the winding streets, we were charmed by the blue and white lime-washed walls and the intricately decorated doors set with brass talismans, tiles and knockers in a variety of ornamental forms. Blue painted pots brimming with bright geraniums sat on the spotless paths outside the houses that had been mostly built by Muslim refugees from Spain in the 17th century. Two young boys were buying bread to take home at a hole in the wall framed by bright blue shutters while cats lazed in the sun, framed by walls washed in yet more shades of blue.

At the other end of the kasbah, is the Café Maure, a popular spot on the bluff with views to the river, the city of Sale and the sea, where the locals take their mint tea and pastries. Busy waiters bore huge trays of delectable looking pastries and pots of tea, beckoning us as we passed through. We enjoyed our tea and the wonderful views and rested for a while. Tempted as we were to linger with a pastry or two, our table at a waterfront restaurant had been booked. We left the kasbah through the tranquil Andalusian garden

Above Left *Wall detail*
Above Right *Kasbah des Oudaias*

Above Left *Andalusian garden*
Above Centre *Cats, Kasbah des Oudaias*
Above Right *Graffiti*
Main *Buying bread*

planted at the beginning of the 20th century – a cool, green public space affording an escape from the bustle of the medina. I wished we could have stayed a little longer to sit and contemplate, like the elderly ladies gossiping in pairs while their grandchildren played in the shade of the trees.

As we made our way to our restaurant on the beach, we stopped to watch the fishermen in their small boats setting off from the river mouth. Dotted along the beach were bait merchants, their wonderful faces etched by the sun and the hardship of their lives, hoping to sell their piles of wriggling worms before it got too late in the day. The coins we offered them for allowing us to photograph them put smiles on their faces as their meagre income was boosted. We spent a good half hour by the estuary, then climbed the steps to the restaurant that was built in an old fortress overlooking the sea.

A table had been reserved for us on the terrace so that we could enjoy the sea breezes. We partook of a very simple lunch of local fried fish and seafood and couscous with large pieces of monkfish cooked in saffron and herbs.

Two youths on the oud and electric keyboard played modern Moroccan songs of their own composition. They had us tapping our feet as we ate and sipped glasses of chilled Moroccan Sauvignon Blanc.

Feeling very mellow after lunch, we nonetheless had to drag ourselves away from our pleasant surroundings for the next stage of our journey.

We drove out of Rabat through the new town, stopping to admire the Royal Palace complex with its spacious parade grounds and ornate metal doors before leaving the capital for the two-hour drive to Fes.

Above Left *View of Hassan tower from Kasbah des Oudaias*
Above Centre *Pastries, Café Maure*
Above Right *Worm seller*

FRIED MARINATED FISH

8 fillets of fish, or the same number of fish steaks, or
small whole fish, scaled and gutted
all purpose flour
vegetable oil for frying

Chermoula
2 bunches cilantro
2 large cloves garlic
large pinch salt
1 heaped tsp sweet paprika
$\frac{1}{2}$ tsp hot paprika
1 tbsp ground cumin
2 tbsp olive oil
juice of $\frac{1}{2}$ lemon
$\frac{1}{4}$ cup water

Carefully wash and dry the cilantro, removing the roots and
making sure all sand is removed.

In a mortar, pound the garlic with the salt and then add the
coriander, pounding until a fine paste is obtained. Stir in the
spices and then the olive oil before diluting the mixture with
the lemon juice and water.

Marinate the fish in this mixture for at least two hours. Drain
well and then dip the pieces in the flour, shaking off any
excess. Fry in hot oil until crisp and brown on both sides.
Serve immediately.

COUSCOUS WITH FISH IN SAFFRON

2 lb thick fish fillets, eg blue eye cod

2 tbsp vegetable oil

1 large onion, chopped

2 cloves garlic, chopped

$\frac{1}{4}$ cup water

2 tbsp chopped flat leaf parsley

$\frac{1}{4}$ cup chopped fresh cilantro leaves

1 tsp salt

large pinch freshly ground black pepper

large pinch saffron

1 level tsp turmeric

1 tsp ground coriander seed

Couscous (**See page xviii**)

Put the oil, onion, garlic and a few tablespoons of water in a tajine or shallow pan. Allow to simmer until the onion and garlic are soft but not brown and the water has evaporated. Add half the chopped parsley and cilantro leaves, the salt, spices and the rest of the water and bring to the boil, swirling to form an emulsion.

Put the fish pieces into the pan and cover, shaking the pan and allow to simmer for 5–10 minutes or until the fish is just cooked through.

Sprinkle with the remaining parsley and cilantro leaves and serve on a bed of couscous.

Gas vendors, Old Fes

3

Fes

Riad la Maison Bleue

DATES STUFFED WITH
ALMONDS

ZUCCHINI SALAD

WHITE BEAN SALAD

SALAD OF JERUSALEM
ARTICHOKES

BASTILLA WITH PIGEON

TAJINE OF LAMB WITH
ARTICHOKES AND GREEN PEAS

Workers' Café

MARINATED OLIVES

SALAD OF COOKED
WILD GREENS

ZAALOUK

BROCHETTES

KEFTA

La Maison Bleue
Restaurant

POTATO SALAD

ZAALOUK OF CAULIFLOWER

SALAD OF COOKED PEPPERS

TAJINE OF CHICKEN
MESSFIOUI

LAMB M'HAMMAR

COUSCOUS MEDFOUN

BASTILLA AU LAIT

Dinner with Younes

EGGPLANT SALAD

TAJINE OF BEEF WITH
QUINCES AND OKRA

TAJINE OF CHICKEN MESLALLA

SWEET BRAEWAT

Above Left *Tiled sign*
Above Centre *Allal*
Above Right *Fatema serving coffee*
Below *Courtyard, Riad La Maison Bleue*

As we entered Fes in the early evening, the sky was already turning pink and flocks of darting swifts filled the sky. The sight of the golden-rose mediaeval city had us gasping with delight but the best was still to come.

Khalid parked the van in a lot by the city walls and we were led up a steep, narrow path lined with mysterious doorways. Soon, one of them opened and a tall, dark and handsome young man dressed in white, with a red tarboush on his head, showed us into a secluded courtyard. We had arrived at the riad La Maison Bleue. The owners, Abdeslam el Abbadi and his son Mehdi were there to greet us.

We were offered rosewater to rinse our hands and lovely Fatema, the maid, dressed in a gold brocade caftan and fringed headscarf, welcomed us in the traditional Berber manner with bowls of fresh milk and dates. In this high-class establishment, the date pits had been replaced with blanched almonds.

We sat on red divans in an alcove of the courtyard, chatting with the owners, admiring the beautiful tiled courtyard, open to the sky, with its swimming pool and orange trees and enjoyed the tranquillity of the evening after our long drive.

Samir, the concierge, showed us to our rooms where we could freshen up before dinner which was to be served upstairs on the terrace with its view over the ancient medina.

A little later, everyone began to emerge from their rooms with dreamy expressions on their faces. What

luxury, what splendor! Each huge suite was imbued with old world atmosphere yet afforded every modern convenience including air-conditioning and cable television. The rooms were furnished with divans upholstered in rich brocades, the brass beds fitted with ornately embroidered linen and the tiled floors covered in Moroccan carpets. Family heirlooms decorated the walls and silver tiered dishes of home-made pastries and large bowls of fruit graced the coffee tables.

In the ensuite bathrooms, pots of blue and white Fes pottery were filled with the local black soap and ghassoul, a type of clay which could be used both as a body scrub or hair mask. Special terracotta exfoliating stones had also been provided for scrubbing one's feet in the same way one would use a pumice stone.

How hard it was to tear ourselves away from the cosseted comfort of our rooms, but the lure of more exquisite Moroccan food was irresistible and, as we were going to stay for three nights, there would be plenty of time to enjoy the amenities of the riad.

On the terrace, Allal and Driss, our two houseboys, served a superb meal. Ten Moroccan salads were offered, followed by a traditional bastilla filled with pigeon and a tajine of lamb with artichoke hearts and green peas. All this was accompanied by two bottles of smooth President red wine.

After a light dessert of fruit salad and a pot of mint tea, we said goodnight but not before booking a scrub and massage with Fatema for the following evening in the riad's own hammam or traditional bath house.

Above Left *Window in suite, riad La Maison Bleue*
Above Centre *Suite, riad La Maison Bleue*
Above Right *Floor detail with Moroccan slippers*

DATES STUFFED WITH ALMONDS

24 best quality dates (medjool or similar)

24 whole fresh almonds

Without spoiling the shape of the dates, carefully make an incision at one end and extract the pits.

Blanch the almonds by placing them in a bowl and pouring boiling water over them. Allow to soak for about 10 minutes and then gently squeeze them out of their brown skins.

Insert a blanched almond into each date in place of its pit and serve with glasses of cold milk.

ZUCCHINI SALAD

4 zucchini

2 cloves garlic, peeled

$\frac{1}{2}$ tsp salt

$\frac{1}{2}$ tsp cumin

$\frac{1}{2}$ tsp sweet paprika

$\frac{1}{4}$ tsp freshly ground black pepper

3 tbsp olive oil

Scrub the zucchini and cut them in half lengthwise and then cut each half into 3 pieces.

Steam the zucchini pieces and the garlic together in the top of the couscousier or other steamer until just tender.

Mash the garlic in a bowl and add the salt, spices and oil. Add the zucchini pieces and stir gently to coat with the dressing. Serve at room temperature.

WHITE BEAN SALAD

$\frac{1}{2}$ lb canellini beans

water

2 cloves garlic, chopped

2 tbsp olive oil

$\frac{1}{2}$ tsp sweet paprika

$\frac{1}{2}$ tsp cumin

salt to taste

1 tbsp finely chopped parsley

Soak the beans in cold water overnight or for at least four hours.

Rinse and transfer to a saucepan. Cover in cold water and bring to the boil.

Skim off any scum that rises to the surface, then lower the heat.

Add the garlic and oil and simmer for about 1 hour or until the beans are tender but not falling apart, and most of the water has evaporated.

Add the paprika and cumin and boil until all the water has evaporated and the spices have amalgamated with the oil to form a sauce. Add salt to taste, cool and stir in the parsley.

SALAD OF JERUSALEM ARTICHOKES

1 lb Jerusalem artichokes

salt to taste

freshly ground black pepper

1 tsp ground coriander seed

$\frac{1}{2}$ tsp sweet paprika

2 tbsp olive oil

Peel the Jerusalem artichokes and cut them evenly into 1 inch pieces. Simmer them in salted water until just tender, taking care not to overcook them. Drain and toss with the spices and olive oil, adding more salt if necessary. Serve at room temperature.

BASTILLA WITH PIGEON

2 squab pigeons, weighing about 1 lb each

$3\frac{1}{2}$ oz butter

2 large onions, reduced to a puree in the food processor

1 bunch flat leaf parsley, chopped

$\frac{1}{2}$ tsp freshly ground black pepper

1 piece cassia bark

large pinch of saffron pounded with 1 tsp salt

1 tbsp white sugar

4 oz blanched almonds

$\frac{1}{2}$ cup vegetable oil

$\frac{1}{4}$ cup castor sugar

4 eggs

10 sheets ouarqa pastry or $\frac{1}{2}$ packet filo pastry

1 egg yolk, beaten with 1 tsp water

sifted superfine sugar

ground cinnamon

Put the pigeons in a heavy pan with the butter, onions, parsley, salt, spices and sugar.

Cover and simmer over a low heat, stirring from time to time until the pigeons are tender and falling off the bone. There should be enough pan juices to cook them. If the liquid dries up before they are fully cooked, add a little water.

While the pigeons are cooking, put the almonds in a small saucepan. Cover them with the oil and heat, stirring until the almonds are a pale golden brown. Drain them immediately to stop them from browning further and reserve the oil. Once they have cooled, pound them coarsely in a mortar or in a food processor together with the caster sugar.

When the pigeons are fully cooked, remove them from the pan and allow to cool. Bone them and tear the meat into bite size pieces. Set aside in a bowl and cover.

Reduce the sauce remaining in the pan until any liquid has evaporated.

Beat the eggs and, over a low heat, gradually pour them into the pan, stirring continuously until combined with the mixture in the pan and soft curds have formed. Turn the mixture into a strainer and allow it to cool and drain of any remaining liquid.

To Assemble

Brush a round tray with a little of the almond frying oil and spread out 4 sheets of pastry, allowing them to overlap the edges. Place another sheet on top. (If using filo pastry, lightly brush each sheet with a little of the almond frying oil as you go). Pile the egg mixture into the centre, flattening it out, and cover with two of the remaining pastry sheets. Arrange the pigeon meat over these and cover with a further two sheets. Finally, cover these with a layer of the almond and sugar mixture and bring up the overlapping bottom sheets into the centre. Then cover with the remaining two pastry sheets, tucking the edges under to form a round pie shape.

Brush the top of the pie with some of the oil and then with the beaten egg yolk and bake in a 350°F Gas Mark 4 oven until golden brown.

15 minutes before serving, turn out and reverse onto a tray and return to the oven to brown the other side.

Alternatively, omit the egg yolk glaze and fry the pie gently in a heavy frying pan until golden brown. Turn and fry the other side.

Turn out, making sure that the almond and sugar layer is uppermost.

Just before serving, dust the surface of the bastilla with a layer of icing sugar and make a crisscross design of cinnamon on top. Serve immediately while still hot.

Tajine of Lamb with Artichokes and Green Peas

4 lb lamb shoulder cut into large chunks

$\frac{1}{4}$ cup olive oil

2 cloves garlic, peeled and crushed

1 tsp salt

$\frac{1}{4}$ tsp freshly ground black pepper

$1\frac{1}{2}$ tsp ground ginger

2 pinches saffron

$\frac{1}{2}$ cup grated onion

6 fresh artichokes or frozen artichoke hearts

1 lb fresh shelled peas or frozen peas

1 preserved lemon, rinsed and pulp removed

$\frac{1}{2}$ cup brown olives, eg Greek Volos

In a casserole, toss the lamb chunks with the oil, garlic, salt, spices and onion.

Cover with 1 cup water and bring to the boil. Reduce the heat, cover and simmer over moderate heat for $1\frac{1}{2}$ hours, turning the pieces of meat often in the sauce and adding water whenever necessary.

In the meantime, prepare the artichokes by removing the stems and outside leaves and trimming the bases. Remove the inside leaves and chokes so that you are left with the whole artichoke hearts. Place in water, acidulated with the juice of half a lemon and a little flour, to keep them from blackening. Rinse and drain before using.

Put the artichokes in the casserole with the meat and simmer for 10 minutes, then add the peas and simmer until all the vegetables are tender (another 10–15 minutes).

Garnish with the rinsed preserved lemon, cut into strips, cover and cook for another 5 minutes. Add the olives and simmer together a for another few minutes. Serve immediately.

Above Left *Perfect poached egg*
Above Centre *Breakfast pastry*
Above Right *Breakfast setting*
Below *Herb vendors, Fes medina*

I awoke to a beautiful autumn morning and luxuriated for a while in the filtered light of my room, wishing I could just stay in and maybe help in the kitchens for the morning. But we had a full day planned so I climbed the stairs to the terrace where the boys had laid out an incredible spread on a white cloth embroidered in green cross-stitch.

There was orange juice, of course, and pots of coffee and mint tea. Eggs, with saucers of salt and cumin to season them, were served with harsha, a flat bread made from semolina. There were beghrir pancakes, slices of French toast sprinkled with sugar, tea cake, sweet semolina porridge perfumed with cinnamon as well as toasted Moroccan bread with butter, orange marmalade and strawberry preserves. Despite my warnings, everyone ate far too much breakfast. Lunch was going to have to be minimal.

Inside the medina, we were assailed by the sights, sounds and smells of this ancient city. Before the shopping bug infected everyone, I thought it would be a good idea to visit some places of interest such as the Museum of Wooden Arts and Crafts which is housed in a beautiful old foundouq or caravanserai where travelling merchants stayed and stored their merchandise. It has a fascinating display of the various timbers native to Morocco with examples of woodworking tools and various wooden artefacts ranging from furniture to musical instruments.

We took our mid-morning pot of mint tea on the museum's rooftop terrace before venturing out, through the carpenters' quarter for an extremely odorous experience at the tanners' and dyers' quarter. This is not for the faint-hearted. Even though we were offered sprigs of fragrant mint to hold under our noses, and despite the amazing sight of the tanners working the skins using methods devised in the middle ages, only Sonia and I lasted more than two minutes. Being a seasoned market haunter, nothing puts me off and Sonia was simply in photographer's heaven. Freshly dyed skins were laid out to dry on the rooftops alongside clumps of wool which would be used for stuffing cushions and mattresses. Skins were being lowered into vats of dye while others were still softening in tanks of an evil-smelling, murky solution whose composition is best left a mystery.

I left Sonia taking photographs of the tanners, joined the rest of the group who were waiting in a less smelly place and made for the shoe market where they could purchase some of Morocco's typical backless slippers to take home as gifts. There were slippers of every possible hue, some with pointed toes and some with round ones. They were made from soft leather, fabric or fur. Some were embossed or painted with traditional designs while others were sequined or richly embroidered. It was almost impossible to choose but selections were eventually made and prices settled.

Above Left *Woodwork museum*
Above Centre *Woodwork museum*
Above Right *Tinsmiths' square*

We had to buy a long-sleeved garment for one of the ladies, a redhead whose fair skin was getting burnt in the sun. I was worried about how she was going to cope in the desert. At the caftan market, she chose a man's djellabah or hooded robe which she donned, looking for all the world like an Ewok from the Star Wars movies, much to the amusement of the local high school students who struggled to conceal their mirth as we passed through the alleys of the souq.

By now Sonia had rejoined the group and we made our way to the covered food section.

The food markets of Fes are a virtual paradise. Stalls were piled high with preserved lemons, pickled vegetables, hot relishes and green, violet and black olives. There were shops that sold nothing but ouarqa – the tissue-paper thin pastry leaves used for making braewat and the extraordinary bastilla. Other shops stocked country butter, fresh cows' milk cheeses in wicker baskets and pots of smen, the salted and aged butter so beloved of the people of Fes. There were tubs of khlea, beef that is salted, sun-dried and then preserved in its own fat, and trays of agrisse, the meaty bits left over from rendering the khlea and which can be used as a stuffing for flaky flat breads. Poultry is purchased live and we saw a man carrying a live turkey slung over his shoulder while a boy weighed a pair of white squawking chickens. On the ground, lay crates of live pigeons destined for the bastilla tray.

Vendors selling autumn fruits and vegetables had set up their carts of squash, cardoons, turnips, okra and quinces, as ambulant mint vendors pushed their trolleys through the laneways. Donkeys and mules bearing heavy loads picked their way through the narrow streets as their owners cried out 'Balek, Balek' to warn people to step out of their way.

On entering the medina, we had noticed a procession of children bearing cloth-covered trays. They were on their way to the public oven with the family's daily bread which would be baked in time for lunch. The baker had a system to ensure that the baked loaves would be placed on the correct trays for collection. It was intriguing to see how much the loaves differed in shape and size from one family to the next.

The troops were really hungry by then so we bought some marinated olives from one of the stalls and set off for a snack bar in the new town, popular with laborers and office workers.

Some of the best food all over the world is to be had in workers' cafés and this was no exception.

I handed my olives to the waiter who put them on a plate and brought us the two salads of the day: zaalouk – a puree of eggplant with tomato and spices and baqoola, a dark green paste of wild mallow cooked with herbs and spices and garnished with black olives and strips of preserved lemon. The house bread was so delicious that we could have eaten it all on its own.

Opposite Above Left *Leather slipper cutout*
Opposite Above Centre *Sewing slippers*
Opposite Above Right *Slipper display*
Opposite Main *Dying vats, tannery*

Above Left *More slippers*
Above Centre *Drying dyed hides*
Above Right *Tannery*

The khlea in the market had given me cravings so I asked for a tasting to be organized for us. A small tajine arrived containing the khlea, unadorned and just heated in its own fat. I was sure that everyone would turn up their noses at all that grease but they were soon dipping their bread into the communal dish with absolutely no shame. It was salty, meaty and absolutely delicious.

The café specialized in brochettes and kefta, skewers of char-grilled lamb, chicken, liver, and seasoned minced meat, so we ordered some of those too. I removed chunks of meat from the skewers with a piece of bread and handed them to the boys before serving the others. It was not often that our guide and driver agreed to join us for a meal so we had to spoil them when they did.

The mint tea served at the end was as good as the rest of the offerings. Restored and refreshed, we set out for our afternoon excursion.

Above Left *Olives*
Above Centre *Pulses*
Above Right *Pigeons*

Above Far Left *Deliverying bread to the bakery*
Above Left *Risen loaves ready for the oven*
Above Right *Baked loaves awaiting collection*
Above Far Right *Taking the bread home*
Below *Transferring loaves to the oven*

MARINATED OLIVES

1 cup mixed pitted olives (green, black, brown)

2 tbsp chopped parsley

1 tsp harissa (or sambal oelek)

peel of $\frac{1}{4}$ preserved lemon, diced

juice of 1 lemon

1 tsp cumin

1 tsp sweet paprika

1 clove garlic, chopped

1 tbsp extra virgin olive oil

Combine all the ingredients in a bowl and allow to stand for an hour or so before eating.

Salad of Cooked Wild Greens

1 lb wild rocket, purslane or spinach
(or a combination)

1 bunch flat leaf parsley

1 bunch cilantro

1 clove garlic

salt

3 tbsp extra virgin olive oil

large pinch sweet paprika

pinch hot paprika

juice of $\frac{1}{3}$ lemon

1 tbsp preserved lemon peel, sliced into
thin strips

handful salt cured black olives

Wash the greens and chop coarsely. Cook them in a covered pot without any extra water for 5 minutes. Cool and squeeze dry.

While the greens are cooking, wash, dry and chop the parsley and cilantro. Pound them to a paste in a mortar with the garlic and a large pinch of salt.

Heat the oil in a frypan and fry the herb paste gently for a few minutes, without allowing it to brown.

Add the cooked greens and cook on a low heat until any moisture has evaporated.

Remove from the heat and allow to cool.

Off the heat, stir in the paprika and salt to taste.

Just before serving, stir in the lemon juice and spread onto a serving dish.

Garnish with very fine strips of preserved lemon and the black olives.

Zaalouk

1 large eggplant

3 cloves garlic, finely chopped

1 tomato, blanched and chopped

2 tsp cumin

1 tbsp sweet paprika

1 pinch hot paprika (optional)

4 tbsp olive oil

$\frac{1}{2}$ cup chopped parsley and cilantro

$\frac{1}{2}$ cup water

lemon juice to taste

Peel the eggplant and cut into cubes. Salt and set aside for 15 minutes to allow it to disgorge any bitter juices. Rinse the eggplant and put into a saucepan with the garlic, tomato, cumin, paprika, oil, chopped herbs and water. Cook until the eggplant is soft, mashing it with a wooden spatula until a thick puree is obtained and all the liquid has evaporated. Stir in the lemon juice and serve warm or at room temperature.

BROCHETTES

1 lb beef or lamb, cubed (not too lean)

1 large pinch salt

$\frac{1}{2}$ tsp pepper

1 tsp cumin

1 tsp sweet paprika

1 tbsp chopped flat leaf parsley

1 tbsp olive oil

Put the cubes of beef in a large bowl and, with your hands, mix them with the salt and spices until they are well coated. Add the parsley and the oil and mix well.

Thread the cubes onto metal skewers, 5 to a skewer. Grill over charcoal until crusty on the outside but still juicy, turning to ensure even cooking.

Serve with bread and Moroccan hot sauce (harissa).

KEFTA

2 lb minced lamb (not too lean)

$\frac{1}{2}$ cup grated onion

$\frac{1}{2}$ cup chopped parsley and cilantro

1 tsp salt

$\frac{1}{2}$ tsp freshly ground black pepper

1 tsp ground cumin

1 tsp sweet paprika

Put all the ingredients into a large mixing bowl and knead to combine well, distributing the herbs and spices evenly through the mixture.

Shape the mixture into sausage shapes.

Carefully thread them onto metal skewers or place inside a hinged metal grilling rack so that they can be turned easily.

Grill, preferably over charcoal, until they are brown on the outside and well cooked inside.

Serve with fresh tomato and harissa sauces, olives and bread.

Above Left *Preparing brochettes*
Above Centre *Skewers on the grill*
Above Right *Cooked Kefta*

Opposite Page *Mixed grill*

Above Left *Unmarked graves, Jewish cemetery*
Above Centre *Graves, Jewish cemetery*
Above Right *Tomb of Jewish martyr*
Below *Decorating plate before glazing*

The mellah, or special quarter where the town's Jewish community was settled in the 14th century and lived under the King's protection, is the oldest in Morocco. It was fascinating to see the particular architecture of the Jewish houses with their balconies overlooking the streets rather than looking inward into an internal courtyard. These days there is barely any Jewish presence in the quarter, most of the community having emigrated or moved to Casablanca since the foundation of the State of Israel, Morocco's independence from France and, finally, the Israeli/Arab Six Day War. The houses are now mainly occupied by poor people from the provinces while the trades traditionally performed by Jews in the past such as gold and silver-smithing and tailoring have been taken over by Muslim artisans.

We visited the Jewish cemetery where the entire history of the community can be read from the inscriptions on the whitewashed graves, some of which are hundreds of years old. We made a donation towards the upkeep of this historic site and chatted to the caretaker about the various families who still make annual pilgrimages back to Morocco to visit their family crypts. He told us that the Jewish population of Fes had decreased from 20,000 at the turn of the century to less than 150 at the present time.

Our last destination of the day was a visit to a ceramics factory on the outskirts of town whose presence was signalled by a thick pall of black smoke issuing from the kilns and clouding the blue sky. Scores of tradesmen were busy mixing clay, forming vessels, painting them and putting them into the kilns for firing. In a special enclave, others carved tiles to obtain special relief effects or chiselled ready fired tiles into specially shaped pieces to make the traditional mosaics known as zelij. The pieces of tile are assembled upside down on a board and cement is poured over them thus creating a panel for application to a chosen surface, be it a wall, fountain or tabletop. It was all absolutely fascinating to watch and we spent over an hour there marvelling at the dexterity of the tradesmen and the beauty of their creations.

We arrived back at our riad in the early evening, tired and dusty. Some of us took a dip in the pool while others had booked into the hammam. I had taken the last appointment and arrived to find Fatema waiting for me armed with loofahs, local black soap and ghassoul.

Above Left *Zelij work*
Above Centre *Etching tiles*
Above Right *Zelij work*

I stripped off and she asked me to lie down on a linoleum mat spread out on the tiled floor. She poured buckets of warm water over me and proceeded to soap and scrub every inch of my skin before massaging me with more of the olive oil based soap. It was so relaxing that I fell asleep, lulled by the sound of the water and soothed by Fatema's strong hands. Eventually, she tapped me on the shoulder, waking me so that she could wash my hair. Swathed in a white robe, my hair wrapped in a towel, I hurried through the courtyard to my room to exclamations of 'Besahtik – To your health', from Mehdi and Samir, the traditional wish to someone who has just taken a bath. I had already learned the appropriate reply – 'Ilah yteik s'ha – May God give you good health.'

I would have loved an hour or two to relax and do absolutely nothing but it was time to head out again for dinner at the famous Maison Bleue restaurant in the el Abbadi patriarchal home just outside the Bab Bou Jeloud, one of the main gates to the medina.

We crossed the threshold into the vestibule and the concierge announced our arrival by beating a drum as he led us into the restaurant.

Mehdi's grandfather, a famous jurist and philosopher, had built the mansion in 1900 to house his three wives and their children. Designed in traditional Andalusian style, its internal courtyard is enclosed and now serves as a reception hall dotted with tables and comfortable chairs where guests can have a drink

before being ushered into their curtained alcoves for dinner. Abdeslam, Mehdi and his sister Kenza, who manages the restaurant, were there to welcome the guests, spending time with everyone and ensuring they were enjoying themselves. A magnificent zelij fountain given to the family as a gift by the King is a focal point of the room and gasps of admiration were audible as each new architectural detail was discerned in the candlelight. The dining alcoves were framed by towering arches of plaster, intricately carved to resemble lace, while transparent gauze curtains afforded a glimpse of the lavishly laid tables and Venetian mirrors on the walls. As we were seated, we noticed that our names had been spelled out in sequins on the embroidered cloth.

Two brightly clad Gnawa musicians, members of a black brotherhood of mystics and healers, played their hypnotic, rhythmic music and chanted, invoking African and Muslim saints, as we tasted each of the offerings brought to our table.

First came a selection of yet more different Moroccan salads featuring whole pieces of eggplant, zucchini strips, cauliflower, carrot, potato, cooked peppers and white beans.

These were followed by a delicious tajine of chicken with a thick parsley sauce and preserved lemon and a simple dish of braised and browned lamb for the meat lovers among us.

Above Left *Entrance, La Maison Bleue*
Above Right *Dining alcove, La Maison Bleue*

The table was cleared and a mound of sweet couscous piled into a tajine, sprinkled with slivered almonds, cinnamon and superfine sugar was presented. It looked just like the dessert couscous we had been served in Casablanca but, as we scooped up servings of the couscous, we discovered that pieces of tender braised veal had been buried within the mound. This was a dish dating back to the 13th century, another of the sweet and savory dishes so typical of Fassi cuisine.

The Gnawa musicians had risen from their low seats and begun to dance, leaping into the air and spinning the tassels on their cowrie-shell trimmed hats, much to our delight. At the end of their performance, they were replaced by a more sedate oud player who interpreted melodies of Andalusia as our dessert was served.

We were treated to the specialty of the house, Bastilla au lait – crisp and delicate leaves of ouarqa pastry filled with a delicate perfumed custard and slivered almonds with a side dish of sliced oranges sprinkled with rosewater, superfine sugar and cinnamon.

I was so relaxed after my hammam and the sensuous flavours of these dishes that I could barely keep my eyes open.

After the mint tea was served and drunk, we bade the el Abbadis goodnight, thanking them for their extraordinary hospitality. Khalid had been waiting at the entrance and drove us back to our riad where we slept soundly between our embroidered sheets until morning when we were awakened by the sound of the muezzin calling the faithful to prayer.

Above Left   *Tables set for dinner, La Maison Bleue*
Above Centre   *Gnawa Musicians, La Maison Bleue*
Above Right   *Main salon, La Maison Bleue*

POTATO SALAD

1 lb potatoes

$\frac{1}{2}$ **tsp salt**

$\frac{1}{2}$ **tsp cumin**

1 tbsp vinegar

2 tbsp olive oil

2 tbsp chopped flat leaf parsley

Peel the potatoes and cut them into dice.

Boil them gently until just tender. Drain.

Mix the rest of the ingredients in a bowl and add the potato dice, mixing carefully so as not to break them up. Serve at room temperature.

ZAALOUK OF CAULIFLOWER

1 cauliflower

3 cloves garlic, peeled

1 tsp cumin

2 tsp sweet paprika

cayenne or harissa to taste (optional)

1 tbsp chopped cilantro leaves

$\frac{1}{3}$ cup olive oil

salt to taste

lemon juice

Clean the cauliflower and divide it into florets. Cook it with the garlic in salted water until al dente.

Drain and mash coarsely. Add the spices, cilantro and oil, transfer to a frying pan and fry until any moisture has evaporated and the salad is coated with the sauce.

Just before serving, stir in lemon juice to taste.

Salad of Cooked Peppers

4 green bell peppers

1 lb roma tomatoes or a can of Italian tomatoes

3 tbsp olive oil

2 cloves garlic

1 or 2 fresh red chillies or dried red chillies

salt

freshly ground black pepper

Grill the peppers and the garlic over a gas flame or on a barbecue until the skins are blackened. Peel the peppers and garlic. Cut the peppers into long slices and slice the garlic.

Blanch and peel the tomatoes and chop them roughly.

Put the prepared peppers, tomatoes and garlic in a pan with the olive oil, sliced red chillies, salt and pepper and simmer for about 20 minutes.

Allow to cool and serve at room temperature.

Tajine of Chicken Messfioui

1 whole free range chicken
(or 3 lb chicken pieces)

2 cloves garlic, chopped

1 bunch cilantro, chopped

large pinch saffron

1 tsp salt

3 bunches flat leaf parsley, chopped

1 cup water

2 preserved lemons

Put the cleaned and trimmed chicken into a large casserole.

In a bowl, combine the garlic, cilantro, saffron salt, $\frac{1}{3}$ of the parsley and the olive oil.

Mix well to combine and rub some of the mixture over and inside the chicken.

Pour the water into the spice mixture remaining in the bowl and swirl to form an emulsion.

Pour it into the casserole containing the chicken and simmer for about 30 minutes or until the chicken is fully cooked and tender. Remove the chicken from the casserole and boil off some of the excess liquid, adding the rest of the parsley and cooking until the sauce is reduced. Cut the chicken into serving pieces and return to the pot to warm in the sauce.

In the meantime, rinse the preserved lemons and cut the skin into strips, discarding the pulp.

Transfer the chicken pieces to a serving dish, cover with the sauce, and garnish with the strips of preserved lemon.

LAMB M'HAMMAR

1 lamb forequarter with the bone (approx 3 lb),
cut into pieces

4 cloves garlic, chopped

1 tbsp sweet paprika

2 tsp ginger

1 tbsp salt

1 tsp smen or salted butter

small pinch saffron

$\frac{1}{3}$ cup vegetable oil

5 stems fresh cilantro tied into a bunch

vegetable oil for frying

In a saucepan combine the garlic, salt, spices and smen and
rub this mixture into the pieces of lamb.

Add the oil, cover with water and add the cilantro.

Simmer on a low heat for about 2 hours or until the lamb
is very tender and the sauce reduced.

Remove the lamb pieces from the saucepan and drain.

Heat some oil in a frypan and fry the lamb pieces until
crisp and brown all over.

Transfer the browned lamb pieces to a serving dish and
pour the sauce over them.

COUSCOUS MEDFOUN

Stew

2 onions, peeled and cut in half

2 pieces cassia bark

pinch saffron

1 tsp salt

1 tsp pepper

1–1$\frac{1}{2}$ lb veal, cubed

$\frac{1}{2}$ cup oil

$\frac{1}{4}$ cup water

Garnish

1 cup fried almonds

1 tsp orange blossom water

$\frac{1}{2}$ cup superfine sugar

1 tbsp cinnamon

Couscous (**See page xviii**)

Put all the ingredients for the stew into a heavy pot or tajine and simmer for 1 to 1$\frac{1}{2}$ hours until the veal is very tender.

Discard the onions. Remove the veal from the casserole and set aside, leaving the sauce behind.

Prepare the couscous as usual. Moisten it with the sauce from the veal.

Arrange half of the steamed couscous in a serving dish. Mound the cooked veal in the middle of the dish.

Cover the veal with the remaining couscous, moulding it into a dome.

Cover it with the fried almonds, coarsely ground and mixed with the orange blossom water, and crown with a cap of superfine sugar. Make decorative designs on the couscous with the cinnamon and serve immediately, with little bowls of extra sugar and cinnamon if desired.

BASTILLA AU LAIT

10 sheets of ouarqa

or

10 sheets of filo pastry cut into rounds
the size of a dinner plate.

vegetable oil for frying

8 oz toasted blanched almonds

$\frac{1}{4}$ cup caster sugar

1 tsp cinnamon

Cream

3 tbsp cornflour

2 pints milk, plus an extra 4 tbsp

3 oz caster sugar

pinch salt

3 tbsp almond meal

2 tbsp orange blossom water

The Cream

In a bowl, blend the cornflour with the 4 tbsp of milk. Heat the rest of milk with the sugar and salt. Add the cornflour mixture and simmer, stirring until the mixture has thickened and coats a spoon. Add the almond meal and orange blossom water, stirring to combine. Transfer to a bowl, covering the surface with plastic wrap to prevent a skin from forming. Cool and then set aside in the refrigerator to chill.

In a mortar or a food processor, coarsely grind the toasted almonds with the sugar, stir in the cinnamon and set aside.

Fry the rounds of pastry, two at a time in the vegetable oil until golden brown and crisp. Drain well and set aside.

To Assemble

Warm the fried pastry in a low oven until crisp and dry.

Place two sheets of pastry on a serving tray.

Spread with $\frac{1}{3}$ of the cream.

Place another 2 sheets of pastry on top and sprinkle with $\frac{1}{3}$ of the almond and sugar mixture

Repeat this process with the remaining ingredients ending with the last $\frac{1}{3}$ of the cream. Sprinkle the remaining almond mixture on top of the cream and serve immediately, before the pastry has a chance to become soggy.

Above Left *Granaries, Meknes*
Above Centre *Tomb of Moulay Ismail*
Above Right *Interior view of granaries*
Below *Poultry vendor*

As we emerged from our rooms we found that the first rains of autumn had fallen as we slept, washing the late summer's dust from the marble tiles in the courtyard and glossing the leaves of the orange trees. Braving the rain, we set out for the imperial city of Meknes.

Moulay Ismail, the second Alaouite ruler of Morocco, notorious for his cruelty and the power of his army, had made Meknes his capital. A contemporary of Louis XVI, he erected splendid buildings, many of which have since been plundered or destroyed by earthquakes. The magnificent Bab el Mansour (Gate of the Conqueror) served as the main entrance to his imperial city, and is still well preserved. We stopped to admire the gate and continued, past the large Agdal reservoir, to the famous granaries where feed was stored for the 12,000 horses kept by this powerful ruler. The huge thick-walled complex had been cooled by underground water channels and, even though the many ruined arches outside were overgrown with vegetation, its sheer scale and grandeur were still most impressive.

We could not miss an opportunity to inspect Moulay Ismail's ornately decorated mausoleum which has recently been restored under the patronage of the royal family and which is open to non-Muslims each day except Friday.

On our way out of the city, we stopped for a quick foray into the medina where we bought some Meknes olives which are reputedly the finest in Morocco.

We drove on to the ruined Roman city of Volubilis hoping that the rain would stop soon. On arrival, we found the site completely deserted apart from a few hopeful boys with umbrellas for hire at the price of 3 dirhams each and the usual postcard and souvenir vendors sheltering under the cover of their stands.

Armed with our hired umbrellas, we climbed a hill lined with carob trees to tour the ruins of the town which dates from the 2nd century AD. The rain had afforded us the rare privilege of seeing the many well-preserved mosaics in their full glory. Usually dry and dusty, it is normally hard to discern their colors which have been bleached by the sun over the centuries. Now they shone, revealing vestiges of their original splendor. The remnants of the triumphal arch and colonnaded streets came alive under the moody light of the impending storm and, just as we were about to begin our descent, lightning forked down and thunderclaps rang out creating a natural sound-and-light show for us. A fierce wind sprang up turning our flimsy umbrellas inside out and bending them beyond recognition.

We sheltered for a while behind a stone wall housing an ancient stone olive press before hurrying down to our waiting car.

Above Left *Pastry vendor*
Above Centre *Women shopping*
Above Right *Nougat vendors*

Market scene, Meknes

Above Far Left *Mosaic , Volubilis*
Above Left *Road, Volubilis*
Above Right *Roman inscription*
Above Far Right *Olive press*
Main *Volubilis*

It was a short drive to the town of Moulay Idriss through hills planted with the olive trees whose cultivation in Morocco was developed by the Roman conquerors.

This town is named after Idriss I, a great grandson of the prophet Mohammed who had fled Mecca late in the 8th century, introducing Islam to Morocco and founding its first ruling dynasty. The town is the holiest in all Morocco as it houses the tomb of this most revered ruler and saint and, as pilgrimage to Mecca constitutes one of the five pillars of Islam, is the next best destination of pilgrims unable to make the journey to Mecca or Medina. Non-Muslims are barred from spending the night in the town but may make a day visit there, although access to the tomb of Moulay Idriss and the mosques is not permitted.

On a previous visit, my driver had led me up hundreds of steps through winding alleys to a vantage point at the summit of the hill where the views were breathtaking. After our trek, we had lunched simply, buying lamb from one of the butchers in the market who had minced it on the spot and seasoned it with onions and spices. We had taken it to one of the cafés in the square who, for a small fee, grilled it for us while a boy was sent to purchase bread, black olives and harissa from the market nearby.

I had hoped to repeat the experience with my group but it was too wet to attempt the climb. I found the butcher but the storm had caused a total power failure and he was unable to operate his mincer. As I was reluctant to buy minced meat that had been exposed to the elements and flies for any length of time, I ordered freshly cut chunks of lamb from one of the stalls and watched the owner season them with spices, oil and parsley. I helped him thread them onto skewers so that they could be grilled more quickly for my hungry group. We devoured them with bread from the market and tasty green olives seasoned with preserved lemons. Mint tea completed our simple but satisfying lunch.

The weather had not improved much so we called it a day and returned to the comfort of our riad to rest and enjoy the tranquillity of our surroundings.

That night we had been invited to dinner by one of the el Abbadi cousins whose family owned a Merinid-style villa deep within the medina.

We walked to the house in the rain, dodging puddles and watching our step. As we made our way through the dark alleys of this ancient city, we felt as though we had gone back in time. There was no sign of modernity – not a soul in sight, no cars, no street lamps, nothing at all except for the cobbled streets and anonymous walls and doors.

Above Left *Volubilis ruins overlooking Moulay Idriss*
Above Centre *Moulay Idriss*
Above Right *Minaret, Moulay Idriss*

We eventually stopped outside a totally unremarkable entrance which opened into an enormous central courtyard fully tiled with blue and white zelij work on the walls and green and white tiles on the floor. It was illuminated by the flickering light of candle-powered brass lanterns. Ornate plaster arches supported by tiled columns led to salons whose doors were fashioned from carved cedar. We were welcomed by Younes el Abbadi, a young cousin of Mehdi's. As his family was still away at their summer house in Tangiers, Younes was our sole host for the evening.

Dinner, he told us, had been cooked by his nanny who had been in the employ of the family for thirty-five years and whose culinary training had been supervized by his mother and grandmother. He had borrowed a waiter from La Maison Bleue and had engaged the services of an oud player to serenade us as we dined.

As we chatted with Younes, five salads were brought to the table which had been set with the family's best china and glassware.

There was a salad of simmered eggplant, another of fried eggplant, a cooked salad of peppers and tomatoes, a puree of green peppers and a sweet tomato jam. Bread was offered from an engraved brass container with a conical lid.

Two unusual tajines followed. The first was beef with okra and a quince-like fruit called l'qem which is native to Fes and has a fleeting season of only a few weeks a year. It was incredibly good, as was the second tajine of country chicken smothered in bitter cracked green olives.

Dessert took the form of three kinds of sweet cakes; triangular braewat filled with ground almonds, fried and then coated in honey, and two kinds of free form cakes known as chebakkia, also fried and dipped in honey, one of which was covered in sesame seeds. These surrounded a mound of sweet butter and Younes confessed that he loved scooping up a little of the butter with each cake before taking a bite. I found this rather excessive but we were obliged to have a taste so as not to offend our host. Thankfully, mint tea was on hand to help digest our meal, although, by this stage, I was supine on one of the couches and didn't know how I was ever going to get up again. It reminded me of our family festival dinners at home when I had to lie down between courses.

This was our final night in Fes and we were thrilled with our dinner with Younes and with having had the opportunity to experience three such beautiful houses, all built in different architectural styles during our brief stay in this ancient town. We left our new friend and made our way home through the dark streets of old Fes.

Above Left *Detail, Younes House*
Above Centre *Zelij and cedar doors, Younes house*
Above Right *Dining room viewed from internal courtyard, Younes house*
Opposite Page *Dining room, Younes House*

Eggplant Salad

4 small eggplants

2 cloves garlic, chopped

large pinch salt

$\frac{1}{4}$ cup water

juice of $\frac{1}{2}$ lemon

$\frac{1}{2}$ tsp sweet paprika

$\frac{1}{2}$ tsp cumin

2 tbsp olive oil

Peel the eggplants and cut them into quarters lengthwise.

Put them into a saucepan with the garlic, salt and water and cook over a low heat until the eggplants are soft and all the liquid has evaporated.

Mix together the remaining ingredients and add the eggplant pieces while they are still hot, stirring well to combine. Serve at room temperature.

TAJINE OF BEEF WITH QUINCES AND OKRA

1 tsp salt

1 tsp black pepper

$\frac{1}{2}$ tsp saffron

4 lb beef shank, bone in, cut into large pieces

4 onions, sliced

water

$\frac{1}{2}$ cup salad oil

2 pieces cassia bark

3 large quinces

1 lemon

8 oz okra

In a bowl, combine the salt, pepper and saffron with a little water. Turn the beef pieces in this mixture to coat them well.

Put one of the sliced onions into a deep pot, then place the meat pieces on top. Cover with water then add the oil and cassia bark. Bring to the boil and simmer for about $1\frac{1}{2}$ hours or until the meat is tender.

While the meat is cooking, wash the quinces. Cut them in half and remove the cores but do not peel them. Cut a cross into each quince half to let the flavors penetrate. Keep in a bowl of water acidulated with lemon juice until you are ready to cook them.

Trim the okra removing their tips, the stems and the tough skin around the stems.

When the meat is cooked, transfer a little of the sauce to a small saucepan and cook the okra in it for about 10 minutes until tender.

Spread the remaining onions over the meat and the quinces on top. Cook for 5–10 minutes until the onions and quinces are tender. Take care not to overcook so that the quinces do not disintegrate.

Transfer the meat to a serving dish. Taste the sauce and adjust the seasoning if necessary. Pour the sauce over the meat and arrange the quinces and the cooked okra with their sauce on top.

Above Left *Quinces and okra*
Above Right *Okra for sale in Fes market*

TAJINE OF CHICKEN MESLALLA

10 chicken thighs, with bone

2 onions, peeled and pureed in the food processor

4 cloves garlic, finely chopped

1 bunch fresh cilantro, chopped

$\frac{1}{2}$ bunch flat leaf parsley, chopped

1 tsp salt

1 heaped tsp cumin

1 tsp sweet paprika

1 tsp ground ginger

large pinch saffron

$\frac{1}{2}$ tsp freshly ground black pepper

2 tbsp vegetable oil

$\frac{1}{2}$ cup water

1 lb cracked green olives

juice of 1 lemon

Combine the onions, garlic, cilantro, parsley, salt, spices and oil in a bowl and mix well.

Rub some of the mixture into the chicken pieces and arrange them in a low-sided casserole or tajine.

Add the water to the remaining spice mixture and swirl to combine. Pour over the chicken pieces and bring to the boil. Cover, reduce the heat and simmer until the chicken is cooked, approximately 20–30 minutes.

While the chicken is cooking, rinse the olives and remove their pits. Add them to the chicken in the casserole and simmer for a further 10 minutes or until the sauce has thickened.

Just before serving, stir in the lemon juice and remove the chicken pieces to a warm serving dish.

Cover the chicken with the olives, reduce the sauce and pour it over the chicken and olives.

Serve immediately.

Sweet Braewat

8 oz almond meal

$3\frac{1}{2}$ oz superfine sugar

$\frac{1}{2}$ tsp ground cinnamon

1 tbsp orange blossom water

1 tbsp melted butter

20 strips ouarqa or filo pastry cut into 6 x 8 in rectangles

vegetable oil for frying

2 cups honey

Combine the almond meal, sugar, cinnamon, orange blossom water and butter in a bowl and knead until a firm paste is obtained.

Place a walnut-sized piece of paste in the bottom corner of one of the strips of pastry and fold over to the right to form a triangle, enclosing the filling. Keep folding, first to the left and then to the right, keeping the triangular shape. After the last fold, either tuck in any remaining pastry or seal it with a little eggwhite.

Bring the honey to the boil in a deep saucepan.

Heat the oil in a frying pan and fry the packages, two or three at a time, on both sides until golden brown. Remove them and transfer them to the molten honey, letting them absorb it for a few minutes, then drain them on a rack and let them cool before serving or storing in an airtight tin.

Above Left *Ifrane town square*
Above Centre *Cedar forest*
Above Right *Cedar logs*
Below *Women at horse market*

It was still raining as we gathered for breakfast early the next morning. We were packed and ready to leave for the long drive over the Atlas Mountains to the Sahara Desert. We bade farewell to the staff, sad to leave the cosseted comfort of this wonderful refuge and promised to return.

We drove in the pouring rain, making our first pit-stop at the alpine town of Ifrane. We could have been in the north of France. The town, built in the 1930s looked for all the world like a European ski village with its wooden houses and shops with their peaked roofs. Ifrane is home to an international university where all courses are taught in English and students from the country's elite are educated. It was quite bizarre to see Arabic signs in these alpine surroundings.

We stopped at a café and ordered glasses of almond milk, buying chocolate croissants for the road, before continuing our route through the cedar forests of the Middle Atlas. I was hoping to catch a glimpse of the Barbary apes that inhabit these forests. These are the only monkeys native to North Africa and can also be found at the Rock of Gibraltar. One can usually spot a few of them waiting hopefully by the roadside for a food handout from passing trucks, but we were out of luck. The rain had driven them to seek shelter in the trees.

As we crossed over the High Atlas Mountains, the rain ceased abruptly and we stopped to admire the scenery and then made a detour to a village where we had the rare privilege of witnessing the annual horse and donkey market in progress.

A few hours later, we arrived in Midelt, a road stop between the Middle and High Atlas Mountains where we lunched on vegetable soup and a platter of perfectly cooked trout from the nearby mountain lakes served with roasted quinces. A young Gnawa musician dressed in red satin played and danced for us and was later joined by one of the local guides for an impromptu jam session.

Above Left *Nomad children, Middle Atlas*
Above Centre *Middle Atlas village*
Above Right *Horse and donkey market*

Above *Gnawa musician, Midelt*

103

4

The Tafilalet

Merzouga

Couscous Bedaoui

Mechoui

Rissani

Medfouna

Mint Tea

Erfoud

Grated Cucumber Salad

Spicy Salad of
cooked Carrots

Tajine of Chicken
Kdra with Chickpeas
and Turnips

Tajine of Lamb
with Prunes

Above Left *Coming home from the well*
Above Far Left *Roadside date vendor*
Above Right *Approaching Erfoud*
Above Far Right *Dates in home-made containers*
Below *Group of women at Errachidia*

106

We made our last tea stop at the garrison town of Er-rachidia before heading south through the beautiful Ziz valley towards Erfoud, a small town surrounded by palmeraies and famous for its dates. Autumn is the peak of the date harvest and, along the way, we stopped to buy some from children waiting for passing trade by the roadside. We distributed the croissants we had bought in Ifrane among them. Further on, there were yet more date vendors, some of them offering their fruit in exquisite containers, hand-woven from palm fronds.

We arrived at our destination at dusk and left our luggage at our hotel as prearranged. Two Land Rovers were waiting to drive us to a camp site on the edge of the Sahara Desert where we were to have dinner and spend the night.

We drove in the pitch dark, our local drivers pulling out and driving on parallel trails visible only to them so that we could leave the windows open and not be bothered by the dust thrown up by the other car.

After almost an hour, we pulled up outside a circle of brown woven tents, the entrance to which was marked by an arch of palm fronds and colorful sequined blankets in blue, red and yellow. A local tribesman clad in the traditional indigo-dyed blue robes, showed us our individual sleeping tents and pointed out the toilet and shower tents. We were then led to an area right on the edge of the desert where carpets had been spread out on the sand and where a magnificent dinner was served.

First came bowls of harira soup accompanied by local dates. This was followed by a huge tray bearing a traditional Moroccan mechoui – half a lamb smeared with butter and spices and roasted for a long time over coals until it was crisp on the outside and soft and succulent on the inside. This is traditionally eaten with one's fingers but cutlery had been provided for our convenience.

Moroccan hospitality, which is legendary, especially in the desert, did not permit the meal to end there. A pyramid of couscous decorated with vegetables and surmounted by a crown of sweet onions and raisins was placed before us and I showed my group how to roll it into balls and flip it into their mouths, as I had been taught. Most of them gave up and resorted to using the spoons that had been provided.

A troupe of white-robed musicians from nearby Rissani played traditional instruments and sang, first circling our group and then settling in a ring at one end of the tent complex where they played softly until we had finished our meal.

As we had been travelling all day and had to be up before dawn, we retired to our tents straight after dinner. Mattresses had been placed on carpets on the ground and clean, white bed linen had been provided.

The silence of the desert hung heavy over the encampment and candles in the lanterns, placed at the entrance to light the way to the ablution tents, flickered gently.

Above Left *Graffiti on road to Erfoud*
Above Right *Campsite at Merzouga*

Above Left *Ahmed with lead camel*
Above Centre *Musicians*
Above Right *Desert dining space*
Main *Camels at Merzouga*

108

This idyllic scene was soon disrupted as men in the neighbouring tents fell asleep and began to snore. It was like trying to sleep in a frog pond, the various snores uniting in a very loud and discordant chorus.

I just knew sleep would not come under the circumstances so I got up and sat on a carpet outside the tents. I plugged into my MP3 player and listened to Moroccan music while contemplating the star-studded sky.

At around 4 am, Ahmed the camel driver arrived with a string of six camels to take us up to view the sunrise. He beat his drum to wake the others and I chatted with him and was introduced to his handsome and sweet tempered ships of the desert while we waited.

The night was exceptionally still and clear and we learned how lucky we were to have such perfect conditions. Ahmed had organized scarves for everyone just in case the wind blew up and we needed to protect our noses and mouths from the fine sand.

As we mounted our camels, a group of tribesmen appeared and attached themselves to each of us, accompanying us by foot on the thirty-minute journey over the sands. We met no one else on our way, enjoying the purity of the air and the brilliance of the stars as we rode. We dismounted and were helped by our tribesmen up to the crest of a high dune where we sat and waited for the sun to rise over the Sahara. A glow appeared slowly over the horizon and we could make out the shapes of the old kasbahs in the distance. These formed a chain of inns where caravans bearing gold and slaves used to stop and rest on their way up from sub-Saharan Africa. As the sun rose higher in the sky, a shimmering lake appeared on the horizon – our first mirage.

We sat and marvelled at the changing colors of the sand and sky and the exotic tribesmen and their camels who cast long shadows on the dunes.

We finally re-mounted and made our way back down to Merzouga, farewelling our tribesmen but not before they persuaded us to buy some of the fossils they had gathered in the desert and lovingly polished for sale to tourists. This was how they made their living and we were only too pleased to reward their patience and good humour with a purchase or two.

We returned to our tents to freshen up and pack before breakfast. Benches in the adjoining breakfast tent were covered in bright yellow sequined rugs with quite a large number of knotted carpets spread out on the ground outside blending into the great expanse of sand. Our host, Hamid had organized fresh orange juice, black olives and a plate of fried eggs and sliced tomatoes accompanied by spongy flat crepes and fresh bread that the Land Rover drivers had no doubt brought from Erfoud with the morning contingent of sunrise viewers. There were small dishes of salt, cumin, green olive oil and fruit preserves as well. Coffee and tea were served and everyone tucked in with relish.

The sun was shining strongly as we reluctantly left this magical setting for the bumpy drive back to Erfoud, passing a few bizarre buildings daubed with wonderful graffiti in which some of the locals had set up stores specialising in the sale of fossils.

Above Left *Breakfast tent Merzouga*
Above Right *Tea and coffee pots*

Couscous Bedaoui

Couscous (**See page xviii**)

Lamb And Vegetable Stew For The Couscous

2 tbsp oil

8 forequarter lamb chops

2 small tomatoes

1 fresh chilli

3 sprigs fresh cilantro leaves

3 sprigs flat leaf parsley

1 tsp ground turmeric

salt

freshly ground black pepper

3 onions, peeled and cut in quarters

2 tsp ground coriander

2 tsp ground cumin

2 medium carrots

2 or 3 turnips

3 zucchini

2 small, long eggplants

8 oz pumpkin

$\frac{1}{2}$ cup golden raisins, soaked in water and drained

2 tbsp honey

In a large pan, heat the oil. Brown the lamb all over. Add the tomatoes, cut in quarters, chilli, fresh cilantro, parsley and turmeric and simmer for 30 minutes.

Cover with boiling water and add the onions, ground cumin, coriander, salt and pepper and keep simmering for 15 minutes while preparing vegetables.

Peel the carrots, turnips and pumpkin and cut into large pieces. Cut the zucchini and eggplant in half lengthwise without peeling them.

Remove the onions from the broth and transfer them to a small saucepan. Add the golden raisins and honey and simmer until most of the moisture in the onions has evaporated and the mixture is starting to caramelize. Set aside.

Add the carrots, turnips, eggplant and zucchini to the broth and simmer until tender. Cook the pumpkin separately in a little of the broth. This is done as the pumpkin tends to cook very quickly and disintegrate into the broth.

Taste the broth and adjust seasoning if required.

To serve, moisten the steamed couscous grain with some of the cooking broth and pile it onto a serving platter, mounding it into a cone shape.

Arrange the vegetables around the sides of the cone and the meat on top. Cover the meat with the cooked onions and raisins. Serve accompanied with bowls of extra broth and some harissa sauce (see page xvii).

MECHOUI

1 lamb forequarter or 1 leg of lamb (approx 5–6 lb)

2 cloves garlic

1 tsp salt

1 tsp black pepper

1 tbsp sweet paprika

1 tsp cumin

1 pinch saffron, crumbled

3 oz softened butter

1 cup water

Wipe the lamb dry with paper towels. Make a few diagonal slashes into the fatty side of the meat.

In a mortar, pound the garlic to a paste with the salt and add the pepper, paprika, cumin and saffron. Knead in the butter, mixing thoroughly.

Rub the paste into the slashes and all over the lamb, cover and leave to absorb the flavors for 2 hours or more.

Preheat the oven to 450°F Gas Mark 8.

Place the lamb on a rack in a baking tray into the bottom of which you have poured the water.

Bake at high heat for 15 minutes, then reduce the heat to 300°F Gas Mark 2 and baste the meat with the juices in the pan. Bake for 3–4 hours, basting every 15 minutes so that the meat doesn't dry out but forms a crisp, dark crust.

Serve on a large platter with small bowls of salt, cumin and hot red pepper for the guests to sprinkle over their meat.

Top *Dunes, Merzouga*
Centre *Fresh dates*
Bottom *Fossil store, Merzouga*
Right *Mechoui*

Sunrise at Merzouga

Above Left *Fresh mint for tea*
Above Centre *Adding mint to pot*
Above Right *Reviving coals*
Below *"Besaha!" - Cheers!*

116

By 9.30 in the morning, we were back at the Kasbah Xaluca, a modern hotel built in traditional southern style with four stylized kasbahs made from rammed earth surrounding a large swimming pool.

My suite was at the far end of the complex right on the edge of the desert. The bedroom, bathroom and a small salon were on the ground floor with a second salon upstairs and a roof deck with spectacular views of the dunes beyond. It was furnished in the most extravagant fashion, using the local black marble studded with huge marine fossils in the bathrooms, the plaster walls encrusted with local pottery. Regional carpets and textiles covered the floors and furniture. The group was delighted with their rooms and marvelled at how amazing they were and how different from the elegance of their lodgings in Fes. We were free to swim in the pool or take a nap until midday when I had arranged to go to the neighbouring town of Rissani for lunch.

Rissani is a small town on the edge of the Sahara where the Alaouite dynasty originated and from where they moved north in the 17th century, overthrowing the Saadians and replacing them as the rulers of Morocco, a reign uninterrupted to this day.

It was market day and the small square was packed. Women dressed in the distinctive black haik or shawl of the region embroidered with sequins and brightly colored wool congregated in groups while trucks offloaded their wares.

On a previous visit, I had met the Alaoui Elmranis, a family of handsome and charming young men who run a chain of carpet stores throughout the region and who carry an exquisite range of tribal rugs and textiles as well as Berber jewelry, daggers and other artefacts. I had arranged to spend the afternoon in one of their bazaars.

We were warmly welcomed, our heads and hands sprinkled with rosewater, and seated on low stools covered in carpets. Aziz brewed tea for us, boiling the water in an ornate copper kettle over a brazier which he revived using a pair of bellows. He took green tea leaves and sugar from engraved brass containers, putting them into the bulbous metal teapots and pouring a little tea into two of the glasses set out on the large copper tray. He then added plenty of fresh mint to the pot and poured the tea in the glasses back into the pot. When he was satisfied with the result, he served the tea, holding the pot high over the glasses as he poured, making sure that there was a fine layer of bubbles on the surface of the tea – a sign of quality.

In the meantime, a special treat – three huge flat breads stuffed with meat, onions and a special spice mix – arrived from the public oven. This specialty, known as Medfouna, is particular to this region of Morocco and is traditionally made by men and consumed at all-male gatherings.

The Medfouna was cut into portions by the very knowledgeable Abdulali, who then gave us a talk on tribal carpets and the textiles of the Middle and High Atlas Mountains as we munched.

Above Left *Donkey parking lot, Rissani*
Above Centre *Boy with rabbits*
Above Right *Market stall, Rissani*

117

Rachid, another charming member of the clan, dressed two of the ladies in Berber shawls and jewelry and the men in blue robes and turbans. They posed for photographs and then we got down to the real business of the day. Carpets were spread out on the floor, admired, rejected or set aside. Once the elimination process had taken place, bargaining began in earnest. When the purchases had been finalized and the carpets were being packed for shipment, the men brought out their drums and played for us. What an amazing and exotic day we had spent. Rachid offered to take us for a quick tour of the market where I could buy some of the special spice mix used in the medfouna. At the spice store, Mohammed, the young son of the owner really impressed me by reeling off the names of all forty-four ingredients in his spice mix. He would not let us leave before tasting his special blend of tea made from a mixture of dried mints and other aromatic herbs.

By now it was mid-afternoon and the market was starting to pack up for the day. The walled enclosure set with palm trees which served as the donkey parking lot was all but empty as traders collected their animals and made their way home. It was time for us to leave too and return to our hotel for the evening.

Opposite Page *Teapots for sale, Rissani market*

Medfouna

Bread Dough

1 lb unbleached all purpose flour

1 lb fine semolina

1 oz fresh or 1 pkt active dry yeast

1 tsp salt

2 cups lukewarm water

Proof the yeast in 2 tbsp of water with a pinch of sugar for 5 minutes or until it starts to bubble.

In a large bowl, combine the flour and semolina and add just enough of the water to form a stiff dough.

Cover and leave for 15 minutes.

Knead vigorously, gradually knuckling in the rest of the water and kneading for about 20 minutes until the dough is pliable and elastic. Cover and set aside to rise for an hour.

1 lb coarsely ground fatty beef

1 large onion, very finely chopped

$\frac{1}{2}$ cup flat leaf parsley, very finely chopped

1 tsp salt

1 tbsp cumin

1 tsp freshly ground black pepper

$\frac{1}{2}$ tsp hot paprika

1 tsp Ras el Hanout (optional)

Mix the ground beef with the onion, parsley, salt and spices and knead with your hands to combine well.

Divide the bread dough into 2 pieces for a large medfouna or into 4 pieces for two smaller ones.

Flatten one of the pieces into a disc about half an inch thick and spread it with the filling, leaving $1\frac{1}{2}$ inches around the edge.

Make a disc with the second piece of dough and place it on top, sealing the edges and shaping the whole into a round, flat loaf.

Cover and set aside to rise for an hour or so.

Prick the top in several places to allow the steam to escape.

Bake in a hot oven (420°F Gas Mark 7) for 30–40 minutes until golden brown.

MINT TEA

As most domestic situations do not allow for absolutely traditional tea making, this quick method will give most acceptable results.

1 heaped tablespoon Gunpowder Green tea (loose leaves)
lump sugar
1 bunch mint (spearmint), well washed

Bring the kettle to the boil.

Scald the teapot and put the tea leaves into the pot.

Pour in some water, swirl the pot and pour it out immediately.

Put a handful of mint into the pot and pour the water over.

Add sugar to taste and allow to draw for about 2 minutes.

Pour some tea into a glass and then pour it back into the pot.

Repeat this process and then pour out a small glass of tea and taste it. Add more sugar if required.

Put more mint leaves into everyone's glass and pour the tea into the glasses to only $\frac{2}{3}$ full.

This will allow the aroma to develop.

According to tradition, each guest is supposed to be offered three glasses of tea.

123

123

Pool, Kasbah Xaluca

Back at the hotel, I watched a local Berber woman baking flat bread called tannourt in a traditional earthen oven set up in the central courtyard. Two fires had been lit, one under the oven and another inside it. The dough had already been kneaded and shaped and was rising on cloth-covered baskets. The floor of the oven was brushed clean and the loaves placed on it, one at a time. As they puffed and cooked, they were turned on their side so that their tops could brown from the heat of the second fire burning against the inner wall of the oven. As each loaf was ready, it was set aside to cool on a bed of palm fronds.

A lavish buffet had been set up outside with various salads and tajines cooking on charcoal braziers. There were far too many dishes to taste so I made a restrained selection of a few salads, the delicious warm tannourt bread, a tajine of chicken with chickpeas and turnips and a tajine of lamb with prunes.

After dinner, I went up to the roof deck of my suite to enjoy the clear night, the silence and a little solitude after another long, wonderful day.

Above Left *Tannourt bread ready for the oven*
Above Centre *Baking tannourt*
Above Right *Baked loaves*

GRATED CUCUMBER SALAD

2 large cucumbers

pinch salt

1 tbsp superfine sugar

2 tbsp orange blossom water

Peel the cucumbers, seed them and grate them very finely. Put them into a colander to drain and press down on them to rid them of most of their moisture.

Put them into a bowl with the salt, sugar and orange blossom water and stir well to combine.

To serve, ladle portions into small bowls for each guest and provide spoons for eating this quite liquid salad.

In Morocco, this salad is generally made with feggous, a pale ridged cucumber with much dryer flesh than that of regular cucumbers.

SPICY SALAD OF COOKED CARROTS

1 lb young carrots

2 cloves garlic, finely chopped

2 tbsp olive oil

1 pint water

1 tbsp wine vinegar

$\frac{1}{2}$ tsp sweet paprika

large pinch ground dried chilli (or $\frac{1}{2}$ tsp harissa)

$\frac{1}{2}$ tsp powdered cumin

salt

freshly ground black pepper

fresh cilantro leaves

Peel the carrots and cut into thin rounds.

Place them in a shallow pan together with the water, garlic, oil, paprika, chilli (or harissa) and a little salt and freshly ground black pepper.

Bring to the boil and cook over a high to medium heat uncovered for about 20 minutes or until the carrots are tender and all the water has evaporated.

Stir in the cumin and the vinegar.

Remove from heat and allow to cool to room temperature. Garnish with the fresh cilantro leaves and a little more paprika for color.

TAJINE OF CHICKEN KDRA WITH CHICKPEAS AND TURNIPS

$\frac{1}{4}$ cup salad oil mixed with a little olive oil

pinch saffron

1 tsp pepper

2 onions, sliced

2 cups water

3 lb chicken thighs

2 handfuls chickpeas, soaked overnight

4 turnips, trimmed

the turnip tops cut into small pieces

1 tsp salt

2 additional onions, thinly sliced

$\frac{1}{2}$ cup chopped flat leaf parsley

Put the oil, spices and onion into a saucepan with the water and swirl to blend. Add the chicken and chickpeas and simmer over a low heat until tender. Add the turnips, the turnip tops, the salt and simmer for about 10 minutes or until cooked but still firm.

Remove the chicken and turnips from the pan, cover and set aside. Add the additional onions and parsley to the pan and reduce over a medium heat until thick. Return the chicken and turnips to the pan and reheat gently in the sauce before serving.

TAJINE OF LAMB WITH PRUNES

3 lb lamb shoulder cut into large chunks

1 tsp salt

1 tbsp ras el hanout

1 tsp turmeric

1 tsp ground ginger

$\frac{1}{2}$ tsp saffron

1 tbsp sugar

2 large onions, chopped

3 cloves garlic, chopped

1 cup chopped parsley and cilantro

3 tbsp oil

$\frac{1}{2}$ cup water

$\frac{1}{2}$ tsp cinnamon

1 tsp sugar

4 oz pitted prunes

2 tablespoons toasted sesame seeds

Combine the lamb with the spices, onion, herbs and oil in a tajine or casserole dish. Add the water and bring to a boil. Simmer for $1\frac{1}{2}$ hours or until tender.

Transfer a ladleful of the lamb cooking juices to a small saucepan, add the cinnamon and sugar and simmer the prunes for 10 minutes until soft.

To serve, place the lamb pieces on a large serving plate. Arrange the cooked prunes on top. If the lamb cooking juices have not thickened into a gravy, reduce them over a high heat and pour over the lamb and prunes. Sprinkle the toasted sesame seeds over the dish and serve immediately.

Oasis of the Todra Valley

5

The Kasbah Route

Aït ben Haddou

Salade Marocaine

Tajine of Meatballs
with Egg

Above Far Left *Oasis, Tinghir*
Above Left *Boy weaving camel from palm fronds*
Above Right *Alleyway, Tinghir*
Above Far Right *Dental surgery, Tinghir*
Below *Tinghir*

After breakfast the next day, we drove through the palm-studded oases of the Tafilalet to Tinghir where one of the Lamrani family gave us a tour of the oasis abutting the town.

We spent an enchanting hour walking on earthen paths, crossing over irrigation channels and watching farmers tending their plots and harvesting fodder for their livestock before loading it onto their donkeys. Many of the trees were still laden with olives and pomegranates. Date palms framed the picturesque beaten earth buildings of Tinghir which all but disappeared into the barren desert backdrop. Just being in this tranquil garden of Eden refreshed us both physically and mentally.

A young boy appeared bearing pendants in the shape of camels that he had woven from palm fronds. We offered him a few coins and some pens in exchange for his handiwork and he deftly made a few more from palm fronds he carried under his arm in case such a sales opportunity presented itself.

At the other end of the oasis, steps led up into the village and we made our way through the old Jewish quarter and into the marketplace where the Tinghir branch of the Lamrani family were expecting us for tea in their shop. We spent a little time there before continuing our journey, giving the group a chance to do a little more retail therapy from a large selection of silver Berber jewelry spread out before us.

It was only a short drive to the shallow Todra river which we crossed into the breathtaking gorge. Groups of Berber families watered their donkeys and posed for photographs while tourists abseiled off the sheer sides of the gorge. After a stroll through the lower parts of the gorge, we were taken to lunch on the covered terrace of a restaurant built into the rock face where we were served vegetable soup and an excellent tajine of chicken with olives. As we enjoyed our lunch, we were astonished to hear the deep sound of an alpenhorn. We spotted the musician on the other side of the river. He played for half an hour, then broke the instrument down into three sections, loaded it into his car and drove off. We deduced that he must travel the world in search of the best natural acoustic chambers in which to practise his craft.

After lunch we followed the kasbah route through the Dades Valley, stopping from time to time to admire the stunning scenery and photograph the many oases along the river course with their palm groves and patchwork of cultivated plots. Women dressed in bright colors were busy washing clothes in the river and laying them out to dry in the sun. Each stop afforded scenery more beautiful than the last. From the road, I noted the different types of fruit trees crowded into small garden plots. There were figs, peaches, plums, oranges, olives and pomegranates – something for each season.

Above Left *Berber woman, Todra Gorge*
Above Right *Hotel, Todra Gorge*

We made our last stop at el Kelaa Magouna, the rose-growing capital of Morocco, purchased some of the products made from the Damascene pink roses originally brought to Morocco by the Turks and refreshed ourselves with mint tea laced with a few drops of the town's famous rosewater.

Just before dusk, we arrived at the restored 17th century Kasbah ben Moro, just outside the town of Skoura. The kasbah, or fortified castle, dominated a hilltop and afforded 360 degree views of the surrounding countryside – a necessity in days past to anticipate the arrival of marauding tribes.

I had chosen this isolated site so that we could have an impression of what life in a kasbah would have been like in days gone by. All power was provided by a generator and there was no electricity or hot water between midnight and 7 am the next day. Candles lit the way up to our rooms on the upper floors.

After settling in to our rooms, we came down and sat outside where tables had been set for dinner.

We shared a simple but beautifully cooked meal of chicken and lamb skewers with salad and then climbed up onto the roof terrace where mats and pillows had been provided where we could lie and gaze up at the inky night sky, thick with stars, before retiring to our rooms.

The next morning, we rose early and drove the short distance to Ouarzazate where the country's film studios are located. The spectacular scenery and distinctive beaten earth buildings are in high demand for historical movies. Films from Gladiator to Star Wars have been shot in the area and there are huge lots with reconstructed Egyptian cities for films such as Cleopatra and movies with biblical themes.

No one was terribly interested in visiting a theme park so we drove on to the famous Taourirt Kasbah which originally housed the Glaoui clan of Marrakech. We climbed up to the various levels, inspecting the maze of rooms where members of the family had lived with their many servants, before continuing our journey to the UNESCO classified Ait ben Haddou, a spectacular group of fortified buildings straddling an almost dry river bed and surrounded by verdant plantations.

There are still a few families living in the village and we were invited to take tea in a traditional home.

We removed our shoes at the entrance as R'qia invited us into the main room of her rammed earth house where we sat on carpets she had woven herself, admiring the views from the window. She offered us mint tea and a plate of almonds and then took us on a tour, showing us her kitchen, an external cave-like room where most of the cooking was done in earthenware tajines on traditional kanoun or braziers. A simple clay oven contained glowing coals and R'qia offered to bake us a loaf of her supple tannourt bread that was rising under a cloth. Savoring pieces of the bread that was ready in almost no time, we inspected the rest of the complex, noticing the metal couscousier set into its own stove and the wooden

Above Far Left *Detail, Kasbah ben Moro*
Above Left *Rush ceiling detail, Kasbah ben Moro*

Above Right *Interior lightwell, Kasbah ben Moro*
Above Far Right *Mats for stargazing, Kasbah ben Moro*

Above Left *Taourirt Kasbah, Ouarzazate*
Above Centre *Ruined kasbah, Ait ben Haddou*
Above Right *House entrance Ait ben Haddou*
Main *Ait ben Haddou*

Below Far Left *Couscous pot on stove*
Below Left *Rqia with freshly baked loaf*
Below Right *Rqia's kitchen utensils*
Below Far Right *Latifa*

137

Woman going to the well

mortar and pestle and other utensils on a shelf outside the kitchen.

A donkey, some sheep and a few chickens were kept in an adjacent enclosure which, in turn, led into a space set aside for ablutions and laundry. Water had to be drawn from the river nearby.

We played with her youngest daughter Latifa for a while and then strolled through the shop-lined main street of the village where shopkeepers begged us to come in just for a look to bring them good luck.

We crossed the dry oued and entered one of the few restaurants in the village where, seated on the terrace, we lunched on more tannourt bread with a fresh salad of tomatoes and a delicious tajine of tiny meatballs and egg. Enjoying the stunning views of the decorated pisé buildings outside, we watched women coming down to the river with their donkeys to draw water, just as their ancestors had done since time immemorial.

Ahead of us was a four-hour drive to Marrakech, via the scenic road that crossed the High Atlas Mountains through the Tizi'n'Tichka pass. The road was dotted with Berber hamlets and from time to time we would catch sight of groups of Berber women dressed in extraordinary costumes of lace in pastel colors and sequined shawls in pink and yellow.

Each village seemed to have a special color and I couldn't wait to see what unusual color and fabric combinations would appear around the next bend. I was desperate to get some photographs but we were going too fast and the women would flee if they so much as caught a glimpse of a camera. The steep, winding roads afforded ever changing scenery all the way to Marrakech, the pink hue of its walls and buildings rendered more intense by the rays of the setting sun. The last roses of the season bloomed in massive beds planted by the roadside and we were once again delighted by the exotic and exciting look of the town and the new adventures it promised.

Above Left *Washing clothes in the river*
Above Centre *High Atlas village*
Above Right *Winding roads, High Atlas*

Above *Roses, Marrakech*

SALADE MAROCAINE

2–3 firm tomatoes

2 scallions, finely sliced

$\frac{1}{2}$ preserved lemon (peel only), diced

salt

2 tbsp olive oil

juice of $\frac{1}{2}$ lemon

Cut the tomatoes into small dice. Add the scallions and preserved lemon.

Season with salt to taste and dress with the olive oil and lemon juice.

TAJINE OF MEATBALLS WITH EGG

Sauce

3 tbsp unsalted butter

$\frac{1}{2}$ cup pureed onion

$\frac{1}{4}$ tsp freshly ground black pepper

$\frac{1}{4}$ tsp powdered saffron mixed with $\frac{1}{2}$ tsp turmeric

1 pinch hot paprika

1 tsp salt

large pinch ground cumin

1 tsp sweet paprika

$\frac{1}{2}$ cup chopped flat leaf parsley and coriander

1 can chopped tomatoes with their juice

Put all the ingredients into a shallow pan. Bring to the boil, reduce the heat and simmer for 15 minutes while preparing the meatballs.

Meatballs

1 lb coarsely ground lamb

1 tsp salt

$\frac{1}{4}$ tsp freshly ground black pepper

2 tbsp pureed onion, drained

1 tbsp chopped flat leaf parsley

1 tsp ground cumin

1 tsp ground paprika

3 eggs

Mix all the ingredients except for the eggs in a bowl and run through the food processor until the mixture is fine and sticky. Knead well and, with wet hands, roll into walnut-sized balls.

Place them in the reduced sauce and simmer for 30 minutes.

Break the eggs into a bowl, add a tablespoon of water and beat with a fork.

Pour this mixture over the contents of the tajine, cover and simmer gently for a few minutes until the eggs have set.

Astrologer's set up, Djema l'Fna

6

Marrakech

Djema l'Fna

VEGETARIAN HARIRA SOUP

SELLOU

KHODINJAL

Douirya Restaurant

MINCED MEAT CIGARS

GREEN PEPPERS WITH CUMIN
AND PRESERVED LEMON

LENTIL SALAD

SALAD OF COOKED CARROTS
WITH ORANGE BLOSSOM WATER

TANGIA MARRAKCHIA

Latifa's Breakfast

MSAMMEN

BEGHRIR

HARSHA

Market Food

BESSARA

SEIKOOK

MARRAKECH TEA

Above Left *Bab Agnaou gate*
Above Right *Courtyard, riad Marrakech*
Below *Bus stop, Marrakech*

  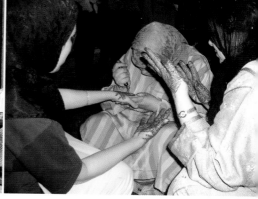

Our riad in Marrakech was butted right up to the pink walls of the medina, just inside the impressive 12th century Almohad gate, the Bab Agnaou. Its courtyard was planted with semi-tropical plants and the swimming pool looked deliciously inviting after our long drive through the barren landscape of the Atlas.

We checked in quickly as I wanted my charges to have their first impression of Marrakech in the crowded, exotic atmosphere of the Djema l'Fna Square on a Saturday night. The name of the square means 'meeting place of the dead' – an appellation dating from the days of public executions when the heads of the executed were displayed in the square.

These days, the square still attracts all sorts of itinerant merchants, storytellers, soothsayers and snake-charmers. At night the place really comes alive with hundreds of food stalls taking up most of the square, the entertainers and musicians working around its periphery.

The food stalls, numbered with prominent signs and lit with electric light bulbs, sell everything from fresh orange juice to snails in aromatic broth perfumed with marjoram and steamed sheep's heads. Most stalls are surrounded by narrow wooden benches where customers can sit to consume their meal.

As we arrived, things were in full swing. Spruikers assailed us, trying to entice us to buy from their stalls.

There were huge vats of harira with plates piled high with dates and chebbakiah, the honey-drenched cakes traditionally eaten with this national soup.

Other stalls offered mounds of golden couscous surrounded by roast chickens, meats and salads.

Young boys ladled snails into small bowls and handed them to customers with a toothpick to extract them from their shells. Others served platters of fried fish and seafood while spicy merguez sausages and brochettes sizzled on charcoal grills.

In the midst of all this color and movement, people were queuing up for glasses of a mysterious steaming red drink, dispensed from an ornate copper cauldron. This was khodinjal, an infusion of sweet spices, galangal, ginger, white pepper, cinnamon, cloves and cardamom infused in boiling water. Reputed to be an aphrodisiac, it is served with a kind of sweet called sellou, also known for its strength-giving properties, made from spiced roasted flour. Two varieties were on offer, one spooned from a mound decorated with sesame seeds and fried almonds and another rolled into small balls a little larger than chocolate truffles.

Above Left *Woman in djellabah*
Above Centre *Café society*
Above Right *Henna being applied, Djema l'Fna*

We made a mental note to return and, after a glass of freshly squeezed orange juice, found a stall with enough room to accommodate us and ordered bowls of harira and plates of chebbakiah.

Nobody was game to try a sheep's head but I hoped we would try more of this magnificent street food in the days to come.

Our dessert consisted of a glass of khodinjal sipped with mouthfuls of sellou and, although I could have wandered around in the square all night, the group, not to speak of poor Khalid who had driven all day, were fading fast.

We decided to call it a night and returned to our riad, leaving the buzz of the square which would go on until daybreak.

Above Left *Watching passing parade*
Above Centre *Setting up for dinner rush*
Above Right *Food stall*

Opposite Above Far Left *Menu, Djema l'Fna*
Opposite Above Left *Diner, Djema l'Fna*
Opposite Above Right *Serving sheep's head, Djema l'Fna*
Opposite Above Far Right *Sausages, Djema l'Fna*
Opposite Main *Food Stall, Djema l'Fna*

149

Vegetarian Harira Soup

4 oz lentils

4 oz chickpeas

2 onions, cut into pieces

3 sticks celery, diced

1 litre water

2 tbsp chopped cilantro

2 tbsp chopped flat leaf parsley

$\frac{1}{2}$ tsp turmeric

$\frac{1}{2}$ tsp black pepper

1 tsp cumin

juice of 2 lemons

1 can crushed tomatoes with their juice

2 tbsp fine semolina

4 oz fine vermicelli broken into small pieces

1 tsp salt

Soak the lentils and chickpeas in separate bowls, overnight. Rinse the lentils in cold water. Boil the chickpeas in their soaking water for 20 minutes. Rinse well in cold running water and rub off their tough skins.

Put the chickpeas, lentils, onions, celery, herbs and spices (except for the salt) in a saucepan with the water and bring to the boil. Turn down the heat and simmer for 2 hours.

Add the semolina mixed with one cup of water, the lemon juice and the tomatoes. Stir well for 5 minutes and simmer for a further 30 minutes.

Add the vermicelli and cook for a further 5 minutes.

Salt and adjust the seasoning. Serve hot, garnished with more chopped parsley, lemon wedges and some dates on the side.

For a meaty variation, add a lamb neck or two cut into the saucepan at the beginning. Remove them and strip them of their meat and return it to the saucepan before adding the semolina mixture. If adding the meat, a piece of cassia bark in addition to the other spices gives a wonderful flavour.

Sellou

8 oz all purpose flour

4 oz sesame seeds

3 oz blanched almonds

1 tbsp anise seeds

$\frac{1}{2}$ tsp grains mastic

1 tsp sugar

1 tsp Ras el Hanout

6 oz butter

$\frac{1}{2}$ cup honey

$\frac{1}{4}$ cup sweet almond oil

superfine sugar

Cook the flour in a saucepan, stirring continuously until it turns a mid brown colour. Then remove from the heat.

Toast the sesame seeds and the almonds in separate containers in a moderate oven, stirring from time to time until they are golden. Reserve a few almonds for garnish.

In a mortar, grind the anise seeds and mastic together with the sugar until reduced to a powder then combine with the cooked flour. The Ras el Hanout can be added at this stage too.

Once the sesame seeds and almonds are done, grind them to a coarse powder, either in a mortar or using the pulse action of your food processor. Add them to the flour mixture.

Heat the butter and honey in a small saucepan until the butter is melted and the two are well combined and add to the bowl with the dry ingredients, stirring to combine and adding as much sweet almond oil as is necessary to form a loose paste.

Mound the mixture in a pyramid shape on a plate or form it into small balls the size of chocolate truffles and place in paper cases. Dust with the superfine sugar. If serving on a plate, decorate with the reserved almonds. In this form it is usually eaten with teaspoons.

Serve with mint tea or khodinjal.

Khodinjal urn

154

KHODINJAL

5 knobs dried ginger

7 pieces dried galangal

3 large pieces cassia bark

6 cloves

10 whole green cardamom pods

$\frac{1}{2}$ tsp black pepper corns

2 tbsp sugar

3 pints water

Place all the ingredients in a saucepan and bring to the boil. Simmer together for 20 minutes. Turn off the heat and leave to infuse for a further 15 minutes. Reheat to just below boiling point and strain through a strainer lined with kitchen paper or through a coffee filter.

Drink hot.

Above Left *Copper urn for Khodinjal*
Above Right *Dispensing Khodinjal*

Above Left *Paving near Koutoubia mosque*
Above Centre *To the oven*
Above Right *Metal workers*
Below *Children in doorway, Marrakech Medina*

One of the specialties of Marrakech is tangia – meat cooked in an earthenware vessel shaped like an amphora. It is traditionally prepared for men by men and is usually consumed alfresco while they chat or play cards. The recipe had been given to me by one of the breakfast waiters at a hotel I had stayed at on a previous visit. I had requested that this dish, which is traditionally cooked overnight in the embers of one of the city's hammams, be ordered for our lunch.

With this surprise in store, we set out on our morning tour of Marrakech. Our first stop was the Saadian Tombs housed in a tranquil walled garden planted with hedges of fragrant rosemary. One of the two mausoleums, housing the tomb of Sultan Ahmed el Mansour, is exquisitely tiled in colored zelij work, whereas the second is more modestly decorated and contains the tombs of his mother and Mohammed el Sheikh, founder of the dynasty.

One can only guess at the magnificence of the adjacent el Badi Palace also built by el Mansour in the late 16th century. It lies in ruins having been systematically stripped by Moulay Ismail in the 17th century and used in building his capital in Meknes.

We continued, through the tinsmiths' square to the mellah, or old Jewish quarter, where the town's Jews had been moved in the mid-16th century. As in Fes, there are almost no Jews left in the mellah except for a few old men tending the synagogues and the Jewish cemetery. We visited one of the synagogues still in use. After a tour of the synagogue and a chat to the rabbi about the history of the community which has now all but disappeared, we made a donation for the upkeep of the site. Blind Reb David then blessed us and our families. It is always sad to see the end of a community and I wondered if there would be anyone to take the rabbi's place once he was gone.

We needed cheering up after the visit to the synagogue and made our way through the cramped lanes of the mellah to the spice market. The perfumes and colors defied description. Each ground spice was precariously piled into a cone for display whereas whole spices, pulses, nuts and dried fruits were heaped into metal drums or woven baskets. The walls of the stalls were neatly stacked with henna used for hair treatment and to decorate the women's hands and feet. There were phials of kohl, the traditional eye makeup made of pounded antimony and natural perfumes of musk, amber, rose and jasmine. All the spices of Araby were here for the choosing. I bought some Ras el Hanout, a mixture of exotic peppers, cinnamon, sweet spices and rosebuds which I grind as I need it to flavor dishes such as the tajine of lamb with prunes or to add to my sellou to give it an even more enticing flavor. There are many myths and stories relating to this spice blend, especially regarding aphrodisiac components such as Spanish fly and other expensive and dangerous ingredients. My mixture, each component apparent, seemed exotic and fragrant enough while being absolutely safe.

Above Left *Metal worker*
Above Centre *Sign in old Jewish quarter*
Above Right *Ras el Hanout*

It was so exciting in the spice quarter that I had to be reminded that our pot of Tangia Marrakchia was waiting for us at the Douirya restaurant in the mellah and that it was time to go.

A low doorway led into a large house that had once belonged to a family of wealthy Jewish merchants. The walls were clad in pink tadelakt, a special Moroccan lime wash, with painted plaster friezes in pastel tones. Vases of pink garden roses graced each of the tables which were clad in gold damask and strewn with more rose petals.

A dish of delicate minced meat cigars served with cinnamon and sugar and a selection of artfully presented salads were brought to our table. The carrots in one of the salads had been painstakingly carved into lozenges and were delicately scented with orange blossom water whose elusive perfume wafted between palate and nostril, barely there but catching you by surprise as you inhaled. There was a salad of green peppers cooked to perfection, the peppers still almost crunchy, and seasoned simply with cumin, olive oil and a dice of preserved lemon.

Then came the pièce de résistance. One of the waiters approached carrying a large amphora, still covered with paper and tied with string. Another placed a heated earthenware dish on the table. The string was cut, the paper removed, and the contents of the tangia, golden with saffron and preserved lemon, were slowly poured into the dish. The pieces of lamb were literally falling off the bone and the meat was so meltingly tender that we used pieces of bread to scoop it straight from the serving dish into our mouths. I thought that it could hardly have tasted better, even eaten outdoors as tradition demands.

Fresh pomegranates, tea and home made pastries were served. After all we had eaten, I could not believe that some of us were lusting after the Bastilla au Lait that was being served to other guests. A neighbouring table of diners had probably eaten even more than we had and their dessert was returned almost untouched much to the despair of members of my group who shall remain nameless. The waiter fetched clean spoons and fed them tastes of the leftover bastilla. I just wanted to disappear from embarrassment, but the manager found the incident quite amusing and, after all, it was a great compliment to the kitchen.

We spent the afternoon shopping in the treasure trove that is the medina of Marrakech. Sonia went off to buy jewelry and I accompanied the others, helping them choose teapots, glasses and trays and even more shoes and jewelry to take home as gifts.

Opposite Above Left *Lemons*
Opposite Above Right *Poultry shop, old Jewish quarter*
Opposite Main *Moroccan toothpick plant at spice store*

Above Left *Entrance, Douirya restaurant*
Above Centre *Interior, Douirya restaurant*
Above Right *Rose petal-strewn tablecloth*

MINCED MEAT CIGARS

20 strips ouarqa or filo pastry cut into
6 x 8 inch rectangles

Filling

2 tbsp oil

4 oz minced lamb or beef

1 tsp cumin

1 tsp sweet paprika

1 pinch hot paprika

3 tbsp finely chopped parsley

1 tbsp finely chopped cilantro leaves

1 small onion, finely chopped

1 tsp salt

3 eggs, beaten

1 tsp cinnamon

Garnish

cinnamon

superfine sugar

Heat the oil in a pan, add the meat, cumin, paprika, chilli, herbs, onion and salt. Cook for about 20 minutes over a moderate heat, stirring well. Pour in the eggs, sprinkle with the cinnamon and cook for a further 3 minutes, stirring constantly. Set aside to cool.

Put one tablespoon of the filling on the lower third of each pastry strip. Turn in the sides and roll up to form a cigar shape. Place each filled cigar on a tray covering with a damp tea towel as you go to prevent them from drying out and splitting.

Shallow fry in hot oil, a few at a time, turning once until golden brown. Drain.

Serve hot accompanied by small dishes of sifted superfine sugar and cinnamon for dipping.

162

GREEN PEPPERS WITH CUMIN AND PRESERVED LEMON

4 large green bell peppers

salt to taste

1 tsp ground cumin

2 tbsp olive oil

juice of $\frac{1}{2}$ lemon

1 preserved lemon

Grill the peppers over a gas flame or on a barbecue until the skins are blackened. Peel the peppers and cut them into long strips and then across into dice.

Toss the prepared peppers with the salt, cumin, oil and lemon and leave for 30 minutes to let the flavours develop. Rinse the preserved lemon and discard the pulp. Cut the peel into dice the same size as the pepper dice and stir through, reserving a few pieces for garnish.

Lentil Salad

4 oz brown lentils

1 onion, finely chopped

2 cloves garlic

4 tbsp olive oil

water

1 tomato, blanched and finely chopped

2 tbsp chopped flat leaf parsley

1 tbsp chopped cilantro

1 tsp ground cumin

salt to taste

Rinse the lentils and set aside.

Put the chopped onion and garlic in a saucepan together with the olive oil and a few tablespoonfuls of water. Simmer covered until the onion is tender but not browned and the water has evaporated.

Add the tomato and chopped herbs and simmer for a further three minutes before adding the lentils and covering with water. Cook on a low heat until the lentils have absorbed the water and are soft, adding more water if necessary. Add the cumin and salt to taste and serve warm or at room temperature.

SALAD OF COOKED CARROTS WITH ORANGE BLOSSOM WATER

1 lb young carrots

2 cloves garlic, peeled

1 tbsp sugar

$\frac{1}{2}$ tsp salt

1 tbsp extra virgin olive oil

freshly ground black pepper

1 tsp orange blossom water

1 tbsp chopped flat leaf parsley

Peel the carrots, cut them in half lengthwise and then across into short lengths.

Put them into a small saucepan and cover with water. Add the garlic, sugar and salt and bring to the boil.

Simmer gently until the carrots are tender but still firm.

Drain and dry well then transfer to a bowl.

Mash the garlic and combine it with the oil, pepper and orange blossom water and toss this mixture with the carrots while they are still warm. Add the chopped parsley and serve slightly warm or at room temperature.

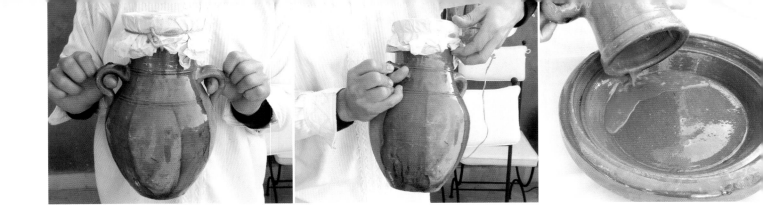

Tangia Marrakchia

4 lb lamb pieces with their bones

$\frac{1}{2}$ **cup olive oil mixed with vegetable oil**

1 whole preserved lemon, rinsed

1 tsp powdered ginger

1 tbsp cumin

$\frac{1}{4}$ **tsp saffron**

$\frac{1}{2}$ **tsp allspice**

1 tbsp melted butter

$\frac{1}{2}$ **pint water**

Place all together in an earthenware pot and cook in a slow
oven (300°F Gas Mark 2) for 3 to 4 hours.

Turn out into a heated plate and enjoy with bread.

Above *Presenting and serving tangia*

Above Left *Pomegranates*
Above Right *Feet and heads for sale*
Below *Sheep market, Ourika*

We had invited our guide and driver to join us for breakfast as we were to leave at 8 am for the Ourika Valley at the foot of the High Atlas Mountains.

Latifa, the maid, had prepared a spread of freshly squeezed orange juice and three kinds of hot breads; msammen, beghrir and harsha, a flat cake of semolina, all served with butter, honey and apple preserves.

It was market day at our destination and we were going to experience an authentic rural market. We wanted to get there early while there was still plenty of action and before the tourist buses started to arrive. As we approached the village, we saw streams of country folk dressed in djellabahs, some with large straw hats, making their way to the market place. Some were on foot, others rode donkeys.

Trucks with open tops were full of farmers with the sheep that they hoped to sell that day.

Outside the meat market, lambs had been slaughtered and skinned, the fleeces lying in bloody piles on the ground. Men stood in groups talking while ewes on leashes suckled their young.

Inside, the butchers were busy gutting, cleaning and carving up the carcases, hanging caul fat and offal on hooks and weighing out chunks of meat for their customers. On the ground, on sheets of brown paper, goats' heads and legs were neatly laid out in lots.

Fascinating as this was, most of my charges found it too gruesome and so we moved into the fruit and vegetable market where the best of the autumn crop was on display – giant mounds of squash and pumpkins, okra and potatoes, carrots and pomegranates were piled up on hessian sacks on the ground.

Stalls had been set up and food vendors were busy simmering tajines, frying sardines and preparing brochettes for lunch. Behind the restaurant stalls was the donkey parking lot. Virtually hundreds of the beasts had been left there to graze and rest until their owners had completed their business of the day.

At one end of the market, merchants sold salt directly from pairs of panniers which had been slung over the backs of their donkeys and were now resting on the ground.

Pots of tea could be freshly brewed to order and the herb vendors were doing a roaring trade in mint and the lemon scented verbena the Moroccans call louisa.

By now, the silver hawkers from Marrakech were buzzing around us like mosquitoes and our guide suggested we take a walk up the hill to visit a potter's house. It was quite a trek up to the house and when we arrived, the potter was not there. His beautiful daughter was busy making bread in one of the outhouses and told us that he had gone to the market to sell his wares. She invited us to take tea with her but we declined, not wishing to interrupt her work.

Above Left *Salt*
Above Centre *Tagine stall*
Above Right *Poultry vendor*

Above Left *Couscous pots for sale*
Above Right *Ourika valley*
Main *Bread making, Ourika*

172

The rammed earth 'kitchen' was spotless with well-scoured couscous pots and other utensils hanging from hooks on the wall. Pots of herbs lined the stairs up to the house which dominated the valley, offering lovely views of the surrounding countryside.

We made our way back down, admiring the pots stacked outside the house next to the kiln and continued our journey into the mountains for tea.

The mountain road wound through lushly wooded hills with Berber hamlets terraced into the hillsides. There were grander houses too, some with 'For Sale' notices on them. These, we learned were holiday houses of wealthy Marrakchis who use them as a haven from the oppressive heat of the Marrakech summer.

We were back in Marrakech by lunchtime and, as we were going to dine at a lavish restaurant that evening, we decided to spend the afternoon shopping in the medina and snacking on street food.

One of my favorite meals in Morocco is Bessara, a puree of broad beans perfumed with garlic and cumin and served with green olive oil, cumin and hot pepper. This, with fresh bread and fried eggs is perfect for breakfast. As we walked through the medina we spotted large cauldrons of Bessara ready to be dished up.

I was intrigued by an ambulant vendor, an old man with a neat white beard to match his cap and jacket, who had metal containers and serving utensils set up on his bicycle. He was selling seikook, medium-grain couscous, steamed and served at room temperature with l'ben (buttermilk). He spooned a serving of the grain into a small bowl and ladled fresh buttermilk over it for us. A few hungry looking waifs were hanging around hopefully so we bought servings for all of them as well.

I was also most taken with a herb vendor who not only sold a whole selection of aromatic green tea herbs but who would also prepare a pot for you to consume on the spot.

I watched him as he brought water to the boil on a portable spirit burner while he prepared the herbs.

I counted seven of them – spearmint, peppermint, sage, marjoram, rose geranium, lemon scented verbena and wormwood. He brewed and sweetened the tea as usual but used some of each herb instead of mint alone.

I found this drink delicious and so soothing that I just had to go back to the riad for a nap before dinner.

Above Left *Vegetable market, Ourika*
Above Centre *Butchers' market, Ourika*
Above Right *Butcher shop, Ourika*

MSAMMEN

1 lb all purpose plain flour

1 lb fine semolina

1 tsp salt

1 pint warm water

vegetable oil

4 oz butter

To Serve

melted butter

honey

Mix the flour, semolina, salt and enough water to make a stiff dough. Knuckle in more water and knead and stretch for about 10 minutes until a smooth, elastic dough is obtained.

Pinch off a quarter of the dough and shape it into a thick rope. Squeeze out balls of dough between your thumb and forefinger the size of a ping-pong ball.

Oil the balls and allow them to rest for 15 minutes.

Melt the butter with 3 tbsp of the oil and a little smen if available.

Flatten each ball into a very thin disc approx 12 inches in diameter. Brush with melted fat and fold a third into the middle, then the next third over it. Then fold in 3 the other way to obtain square parcels. Rest them for 10 minutes before flattening again into 8 inch squares and cooking on a hot griddle or ungreased non-stick frying pan until mottled brown both sides.

Serve with melted butter and honey.

Above Left   *Preparing msammen dough*
Above Centre   *Flattening the oiled dough balls*
Above Right   *Cooking the msammen*

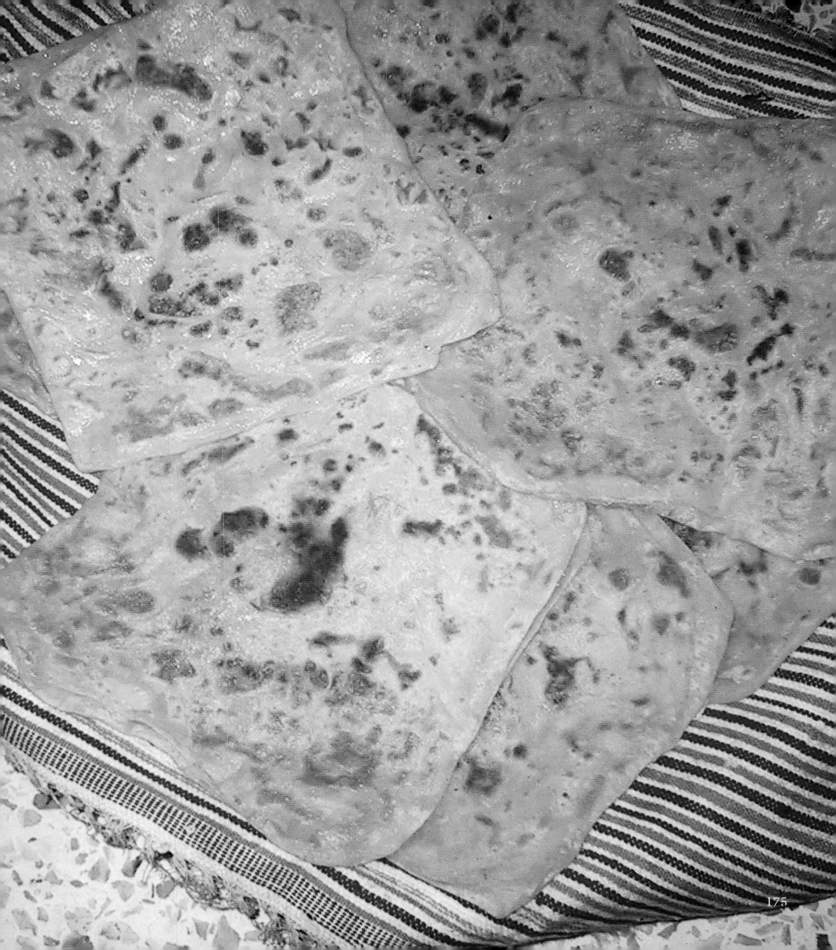

BEGHRIR

8 oz all purpose flour

8 oz fine semolina

1½ pints tepid water

1 tbsp fresh yeast

1 sachet dry yeast

pinch salt

Combine the flour, semolina and salt in a large bowl. Make a well in the centre and add both kinds of yeast and a little water to dissolve the yeast. Stir, adding enough water to make a batter the consistency of whipping cream.

Set aside to rest for 15 minutes then blend in a food processor to make the batter smooth and lump free. Set aside to rest for a further 15 minutes before making the crepes.

Heat a non-stick pan and gently pour in a generous ladleful of the mixture to form a pancake about 15 cm in diameter. Cook over a medium heat until the pancake is slightly colored on the bottom and the top is completely covered in burst bubbles like a crumpet. Turn and cook for a few seconds to dry the top surface and turn out onto a tray covered with a cloth. Repeat until all the batter has been used.

Serve hot or warm with butter and honey or home-made preserves.

Above Left   *Mixing the batter*
Above Centre   *Ladling the batter into a frypan*
Above Right   *Cooking the Beghrir*

Harsha

1 sachet active dry yeast ($\frac{1}{4}$ oz)

1 tsp sugar

1 lb fine semolina

1 tsp salt

$\frac{1}{2}$ pint warm water

Dissolve the yeast and the sugar in 4 tbsp warm water and set aside for 5 minutes until it bubbles.

Mix the semolina with the salt in a large bowl, make a well in the centre and pour in the risen yeast and a little of the warm water. Mix well and knead, adding just enough water to make a firm dough.

Knead for 10–15 minutes until the dough is smooth and elastic.

Divide into 4 portions and roll each into a ball.

Dust with extra semolina, cover with a cloth and set aside to rise in a warm place for 1–2 hours or until the balls have doubled in size.

Preheat the oven to 350°F Gas Mark 4.

Flatten the balls of dough into discs 1 inch thick, prick them with a fork at regular intervals and bake for 30–40 minutes or until light golden brown. Cool on a rack before serving.

Bessara

1 lb dried broad beans

6 cloves garlic, peeled

salt

extra virgin olive oil

ground cumin

hot pepper

Soak the broad beans overnight. The next morning, remove their tough skins.

Put the cleaned broad beans with the garlic in a saucepan, cover with fresh water and bring to the boil.

Skim any scum that rises to the surface and simmer for an hour or until the broad beans are soft and starting to fall apart.

Stir well with a wooden spoon, scraping the bottom of the pot to make sure that they do not stick and burn, mash them against the sides of the pot until a thick puree is obtained.

Stir in $\frac{1}{4}$ cup of olive oil, salt to taste and 1 tbsp cumin and cook for a further five minutes.

Serve in small soup bowls. Pour another tablespoon of oil onto the surface of each bowl of bessara, sprinkle with extra ground cumin and serve with hot pepper or chilli on the side.

Fresh bread and fried eggs make this a filling and satisfying meal.

Above *Peeling garlic for Bessara*

Seikook

Couscous (**See page xviii**)

2 pints buttermilk

Prepare the couscous in the usual manner.

After its final steaming, mix in the butter as usual and allow to cool.

Aerate the couscous, rubbing it with the palms of your hands to loosen and separate the grains.

For each serving, half fill a rice bowl with the couscous and cover it with the buttermilk.

Eat with a spoon.

Above Left *Seikook vendor*
Above Right *Ladling buttermilk*

Marrakech Tea

1 heaped tablespoon Gunpowder Green tea (loose leaves)

lump of sugar

1 small bunch mint (spearmint), well washed

3 sprigs peppermint

3 sprigs lemon scented verbena

2 sprigs wormwood

2 sprigs sweet marjoram

2 or 3 leaves rose scented geranium

2 sprigs sage

Bring the kettle to the boil.

Scald the teapot and put the tea leaves into the pot.

Pour in some water, swirl the pot and pour it out immediately.

Put a the herbs into the pot and pour the water over them.

Add sugar to taste, stir and allow to draw for about 2 minutes.

Pour some tea into a glass and then pour it back into the pot.

Repeat this process and then pour out a small glass of tea and taste it. Add more sugar if required.

Pour into tea glasses to $\frac{2}{3}$ full in order to allow the aroma to develop.

Fishing boats, Essaouira port

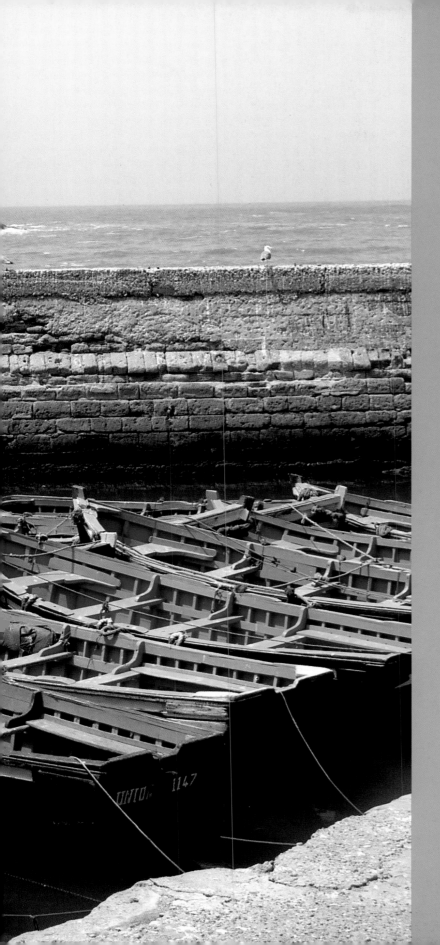

7

Essaouira

Tomato and Onion Salad

Grilled Sardines

Grilled Calamari

Grilled Fish

Amlou Paste

Above Left *Goatherd*
Above Centre *Fishing nets for sale*
Above Right *Shoe stall, rural market*
Below *Goats in argan tree*

Today was our last full day in Morocco and we were going to end the tour as we had begun it, by the sea. Our destination was the port of Essaouira, on the central Atlantic coast to the west of Marrakech.

We set off, driving through miles of vines and orchards of pomegranate trees, to the town of Chichoua, renowned for its colorful knotted carpets.

A little further on, we stopped by the roadside where goats could be seen grazing peacefully up in the branches of what looked like spiky olive trees but which were in fact argan trees. The goats are apparently so fond of the argan fruit, which only grows in this region of Morocco, that they leap up onto the branches to eat them. Little did we know that these goats were actually helping produce a local delicacy! The kernel of the argan fruit is extremely hard and is discarded by the goats after they eat the surrounding flesh. Women gather the kernels and painstakingly crack them, extracting the nuts inside, roasting and then grinding them to obtain argan oil which is prized for its fine flavor and goodness. As well as being used in cooking, the oil is also used as a component in cosmetics and is reputedly very effective in reducing wrinkles.

The Berbers also use the oil to make a paste called amlou, combining it with ground almonds and honey. They eat it with bread, much as we would eat peanut butter. I was looking forward to buying it in the market at Essaouira for our farewell breakfast the following day.

A few kilometres further on, the Tuesday market of Tlata Henchane was in full swing so we got off to see what was happening there. This was another authentic rural market. Piles of everything imaginable seemed to be for sale. There were fishing nets, lengths of rope, old bicycle tyres and lots of dusty old shoes, all of which were missing their laces. There was no shortage of livestock or fruit and vegetables, everything laid out on the ground under shade cloths for protection against the blazing sun. Cones of sugar and bags of salt were also on offer and the old water-seller dressed in his distinctive attire seemed to be doing good business.

The tea stall and harira vendor with his rusty looking drums of soup were getting ready for the lunchtime rush. At a second-hand book stall, a young boy of nine or ten longingly leafed through a French body building magazine dreaming of the day when he too would show off bulging pectorals and biceps like the Mr Universe look-alikes he so admired.

We continued on our way and soon saw the white town of Essaouira gleaming in the distance.

Originally known as Mogador, Essaouira is built on

Above Left *Arriving at rural market*
Above Centre *Rope stall*
Above Right *Magazine stall*

189

Above Left *Entrance to Essaouira Medina*
Above Centre *Orange juice stall*
Above Right *Petits taxis, Essaouira*
Main *Overlooking Atlantic Ocean*

JUS OORANGE

190

the site of an ancient Phonecian settlement. The Portuguese occupied the city in the 15th century and the fortified ramparts that enclose the city today are a legacy of their relatively short stay.

Essaouira came into its own during the 18th century when, under Alaouite rule, it was turned into a trading city with an important foreign and Jewish population contributing to its prosperity through trade with Europe. The town is also the headquarters of the various brotherhoods of Gnawa mystics whose music we had enjoyed in both Fes and Marrakech. An annual festival of Gnawa music is held in Essaouira each June.

On our way into the medina, we passed carts of mint vendors and walked through the picturesque blue and white streets of the walled city in search of authentic high-quality argan oil and amlou paste.

I asked the salesman in the music store where we stopped to buy some Gnawa music if he knew where we could buy good argan oil and he generously led us to a hole in the wall where, he assured us, we could buy the genuine article for a very reasonable price and so we did.

Mission accomplished, we strolled through the spice market where I bought some special spice mix for fish and was offered some cantharides or Spanish fly, a small iridescent beetle which, when pounded into the

famous Ras el Hanout spice mix, is reputed to be an aphrodisiac. In reality, it is an irritant of the urinary tract and can be quite dangerous if used in anything but minute quantities.

We passed through the fish market where piles of glistening sardines, fresh from the boats, were on sale and through streets of antique dealers and carpet shops. Particular to Essaouira are the carpenters and craftsmen working the fragrant thuya wood which is much sought after when carved into ornamental objects, chess sets and inlaid furniture.

A visit to the port before lunch was next. We climbed up the stairs of the Sqala du Port or Bastion from where there were wonderful views of the whitewashed buildings of Essaouira on one side and bright blue fishing boats on the other. Down at the port, the fleet was in and tons of sardines were being sorted, cleaned, bought and sold.

The sea front was lined with stalls offering a wide selection of gleaming fresh fish and seafood including lobster, crab, squid and scampi. Plumes of smoke rose up from the charcoal grills as the stall owners vied with each other for our custom. Khalid was in charge of choosing the stall and selecting the seafood for our lunch. He seated us at a table laid with a blue and white striped ciré cloth and went to make his selection from the day's catch.

Bread, hot sauce and the ubiquitous sliced tomato

Above Left *Mint vendor*
Above Centre *Jars for sale*
Above Right *Musicians, Essaouira*

and onion salad soon appeared with a plate of boiled shrimp. Next came sardines followed by pieces of squid and different kinds of fish, simply char-grilled and served with wedges of lemon, all arranged on artistically chipped Chinese plates.

As we ordered our mint tea, a young man appeared bearing a wooden tray of Moroccan pastries which he was hawking among the tables. We purchased a 'gazelle's horn' each for dessert.

After our fresh and delicious lunch and before our drive back to Marrakech, a promenade along the beach was in order. Young boys were surfing and playing soccer on the sand and we envied their seemingly inexhaustible energy.

Replete and tired by our walk in the sea air, we slept most of the way back in the bus although I managed to wake up in time to make a stop at a roadside stall to buy baskets of ripe pomegranates and purple grapes.

As the group was leaving the following morning, we had arranged for our favorite dishes – lamb and prune tajine and chicken with lemon and olives – to be cooked for us in the riad that night. We would have the grapes and pomegranates for our dessert.

Above Left *Medina scene*
Above Centre *Sardine vendor*
Above Right *Sardines for sale*

Above Left *Portuguese cannons*
Above Centre *Fishing boats*
Above Right *View of Essaouira from Bastion*
Main *Fishing boat marina*

193

TOMATO AND
ONION SALAD

3 or 4 large firm tomatoes
1 white onion
sea salt
freshly ground black pepper
extra virgin olive oil (or argan oil if you can find it)
juice of $\frac{1}{2}$ lemon

Slice the tomatoes and arrange them in one layer on a flat plate.

Sprinkle them with the salt and pepper.

Peel the onion and cut it in half. Slice across to form thin half rings.

Arrange these on top of the tomatoes. Drizzle over the oil and lemon juice and serve.

196

GRILLED SARDINES

1 lb fresh sardines

olive oil

sea salt

lemon wedges

Scale the sardines and gut them, leaving them whole.

Brush them with olive oil and grill quickly over charcoal or under a domestic griller until they are cooked through and the skins are slightly charred. Sprinkle with sea salt and serve with wedges of lemon.

GRILLED CALAMARI

2 or 3 fresh medium-sized calamari

olive oil

sea salt

lemon wedges

Clean the calamari and cut their sacs into bite size pieces. Cut the wings in two and divide the tentacles into groups of 3, cutting the two long ones into 3 pieces each.

Sprinkle with salt and toss in olive oil before grilling quickly over charcoal or under a domestic griller, turning once, until they are opaque. This should only take 3 or 4 minutes.

Serve with lemon wedges.

GRILLED FISH

6 fresh fish weighing about 8 oz each

olive oil

sea salt

lemon wedges

Scale and gut the fish and remove their heads, otherwise leaving them whole.

Sprinkle with salt and toss in olive oil before grilling over charcoal or under a domestic griller, for about 5 minutes on each side turning once, until they are cooked through.

Serve with lemon wedges.

AMLOU PASTE

8 oz blanched almonds

$\frac{1}{4}$ **cup honey**

$\frac{1}{2}$ **cup argan oil or sweet almond oil**

Toast the almonds in the oven until golden brown. Cool and pound in a mortar until a paste is obtained.

Stir in the honey and then the oil. Store in a jar.

Serve with bread as a spread.

Unripe argan fruit

Latifa pouring tea

We woke early the next morning and met in the courtyard for breakfast where Latifa had set our table with our favorite breads and preserves as well as the rare argan oil and amlou paste we had bought in Essaouira the day before.

Our magical holiday in Morocco was almost over and, as a fitting end, I had organized a brief tour through the gardens of Marrakech by horse-drawn carriage.

Our driver, Karim, presented his two horses – Renault and Peugeot – and we set off at a leisurely pace to the Menara garden with its large pool and peaceful pavilions, the Atlas Mountains forming a stunning backdrop to this tranquil haven.

We continued through the French quarter of Hivernage to the Majorelle gardens, set out in the 1920s by the French artist Jacques Majorelle. Now owned by Yves Saint Laurent, it is a spectacular enclave planted with exotic groves of bamboo, palms and cacti with lily ponds containing brightly colored fish and terrapins. Bird life abounds and the buildings painted in vibrant Majorelle blue – the cobalt of French workmen's overalls – is breathtaking and perfectly set off by bridges and decorative plasterwork colored pale blue, green and mauve. That morning, the gardens were full of kindergarten children with their teachers. They were adorable in bright outfits, chattering excitedly like little birds.

We continued to Majorelle's old studio in the grounds, now converted into a small but exquisite museum of Islamic art which houses Saint Laurent's private collection of North African art and craft. The collection of Tuareg jewelry is particularly impressive.

Before we knew it, the time had come to return to our riad where Khalid was waiting to drive the group to the airport and, over our last pot of mint tea to which we were now all addicted, we reluctantly said our goodbyes, everyone vowing to come back soon to do it all again.

Above Left *Pavilion, Menara*
Above Centre *Cactus plantation, Majorelle Garden*
Above Right *Lily pond, Majorelle Garden*

Above *Roses, Marrakech*

Recommended Reading

Cookbooks

Paula Wolfert	Couscous and Other Good Food from Morocco (Harper & Row, NY, 1973)
Robert Carrier	Taste of Morocco (Arrow Books, London, 1987)
Kitty Morse	Come with Me to the Kasbah (Editions SERAR, Casablanca, 1989)
Z Guinaudeau	Fes vu Par Sa Cuisine (J.E. Laurent, Rabat, 1958)

Novels

Amin Maalouf	Leon the African (trans. Peter Sluglett, Abacus Books, 1988)
Paul Bowles	The Spider's House (Black Sparrow Press, California, 1999)
Fatima Mernissi	Dreams of Trespass (Perseus Books, 1994)
Gavin Maxwel	Lords of the Atlas: The Rise and Fall of the House of Glaoua 1893–1956 (E.P. Dutton, 1966)

Reference

Barrie Kerper	The Collected Traveller – Morocco (Three Rivers Press, New York, 2001)

Index
Page numbers in **bold** refer to recipes, those in *italic* refer to illustrations.

The Crew

Seddik

Khalid

Azim & Mourad

Sonia

Abdel'adim & Meera